THE TRAGIC LIFE OF A BLACK LA COP

Truth 4 Change

THE TRAGIC LIFE OF
A BLACK LA COP
Truth 4 Change

RIOTS * DORNER * INJUSTICE * REFORM * PEREZ * PTSD

JOE JONES

Versatile Productions LLC

Published and Distributed by
Versatile Publishing
309 E Hillcrest Blvd
Inglewood, California 90301
Phone: 310-880-5940
Email: versatileproductionsllc@gmail.com

Cover design: Design Solutions 101

ISBN: 978-1-7363288-0-4

First printing: April 2021

In Memory and Honor of

*Deceased SWAT Officer Randall Simmons &
Officer Kevin Gaines*

*Deceased Citizens Rodney King, George Floyd & other
victims of unjustified deaths and incarceration of Blacks*

CONTENTS

FOREWORD

It is with great pleasure that I introduce a friend and confidant, Mr. Joe Jones. While Joe was at Wilshire, I was assigned to the South East station back in the late 80s and early 90s. Joe was a capable young officer who grew up on the streets of Los Angeles and possessed a different optic when it came to viewing himself and the community he lived in. He has always felt that marginalized communities could be best served by police officers who represented the same community and felt a certain kindred spirit.

As young police officers, he and I witnessed firsthand the egregious conditions that were the result of drugs, gangs, and community blight. He would often share his patrol experiences with me, and I would likewise. I learned early on that Joe had little to no patience with any hint of racism, discrimination, or police brutality.

This book will keep you engaged as he takes you through his journey as a son, father, confidant, and a Los Angeles police officer. Even though Joe decided to cut his career short, for reasons explained in this book, he remained committed to being the change he desired for himself and others during these uncertain times. As a reader, you are afforded his optical perception as he shares what it is like to patrol the streets of Los Angeles as a Black man who happens to be a police officer. He leaves nothing to the imagination but gives it to you straight without a chaser. He is unapologetic as he dogmatically reveals his truth. Here is the literary footprint of one of LA's finest: Joe Jones.

Stinson Brown
Retired Senior Lead Police Officer

I have had the privilege of knowing Joe Jones Jr. for over thirty years. Joe is an extremely loyal person who stands up for what he believes in no matter the cost. He is a hardworking and goal-oriented individual who achieves each goal he has set for himself, and as a family man, he has raised two successful sons. I look forward to reading and learning more about him from his new book. I am certain that I, as well as others, will find this book very interesting.

Dennis A. Watsabaugh
Owner of DAW Project Management, LLC/Friend

Get this book! Joe Jones delivers hard-hitting truths about the internal prejudice and racism within the Los Angeles police force ranks. Jones, a former police officer, shares the real and continuous effects of the police departments' retaliation against African American officers.

Michael Brox
Retired LA Detective Public Speaker,
Published Author, "Being Black N Blue"

As someone who was born and raised in South Central Los Angeles in the 1980s, when Bloods and Crips street gangs first got the attention of the world, when 'drive-bys' became common everyday language, crack cocaine first began its horrible reign of destruction in all Black communities, and hip-hop was first created in the streets of LA, which meant a whole generation of young Black people were beginning to move to their own beat. During the same time, LA's professional sports teams in the city began to thrive. This was both the greatest and deadliest decade for young Blacks in Los Angeles.

In all my years of navigating the terrain of the streets, I crossed paths with a few trailblazers whose journey included surviving the 'South Central LA Experience.' One of those legendary Black men is Joe Jones.

Joe Jones' riveting depiction of life as a police officer at a time when fellow officer Christopher Dorner released a manifesto that shook up the department from the inside and created widespread panic, in which lives were lost, will make anyone reading his book question their own boundaries as it specifically pertains to loyalty, trust, and morality.

Folks may not remember, but Joe also released his own manifesto about the LA Police Department. The difference between Jones and Dorner is that Jones is still alive to talk about it, and he does just that by going into great detail in this book! Even for that portion of the book alone, it qualifies Jones' book as a Must Read.

There's a storm brewing, and folks might want to get prepared! In other words, learn all the details for yourself before 'the spin doctors' weave a totally different tale. You've been warned! This may be the most dangerous book you read based on real-life experiences in our lifetime!

General Jeff
West Coast Hip-Hop Pioneer (1975–present)
Skid Row Community Activist (2006–present)

INTRODUCTION

I hope to develop an understanding with you before you begin to read. I am not here to impress you as a writer. However, I have a strong need and desire to tell my story. If you desire to be critical of storylines, theatrics, and grammatical structure, you may miss the point. I am simply a moderately educated man who has experienced some joy in serving his community. Unfortunately, the tragedies and injustice I have experienced have compelled me to share with the world in hopes of curing my heart, my mind and helping those who may benefit from some of the true stories I will tell.

I talk a little about my childhood and some of my life before becoming an officer, so you can know more about the man I became. I was not some corny guy who needed to be a police officer to boost his ego. I was very confident, and I had a good life, a happy life. Moving forward, I will do my best to respect the department and have changed names to protect the identities of many. Trust that I have documents to prove anything I say in my story and understand that there is a reason if certain items were overlooked. Either way, there is no way I could give complete detail of all that occurred as there is too much to remember. So here we go.

Over the years as an officer, I never took any bribe, I never wrote one false citation, and I never hurt, beat, or harmed anyone under the color of authority. Before becoming a police officer, I could count on one hand the times that I cried out of pure emotion. However, I write this book with tears behind my afflictions and a burning desire to release the pressures of my past while revealing the truth of the things that can happen to law-abiding officers, who have a responsibility to tell the truth, even if it involves their brothers in blue.

When communities talk about defunding the police, I implore everyone to understand what police officers encounter that contributes to the safety of the citizens of this great nation. Police officers deal with heavily armed criminals, so they need as much firepower and resources as possible since they have an obligation to the citizens they swore to protect. We should not expect them to do it at a disadvantage. At the same time, reform of the organization to avoid what is now deemed inevitable and unnecessary atrocities is essential.

The behavior of some officers causes so much trauma to the lives of many, and my pain stems from knowing that outside of my personal encounters, countless other Black men and countless Americans have been victimized for no verified reason. Many say, "Comply!" or "Don't make them feel threatened!" or "Look a particular way!" or "Don't put yourself in certain situations!" However, I am an example of someone who would be considered a victim of police misconduct as a teenager, as an educated and well-presented Black businessman, as a naturally large Black man, as a police officer, and now as a retired police officer. However, I humbly accept responsibility for a small portion of some of the things I experienced due to being fed-up with mistreatment. No one wants trouble with the law, not even a police officer.

My broad experiences should give me a vantage point of credibility when I speak. I still happen to have police officer friends, whom I love dearly, and I know that they would not partake in egregious behavior. On the contrary, I know for a fact that there are police officers and sheriffs that have such a hateful nature that they wake-up in the morning with an intent to figure out who they will screw or victimize next! Whether it is their ego, a power trip, or the work of the devil…they do what they do!

Now, this…Black men are dying at the hands of overzealous officers without appropriate justification, and our justice system finds ways to protect the actions of the wrongdoers instead of holding them accountable. Sadly, it is apparent that the government would rather allow the killings to go unfairly adjudicated than to find fault with the officers and have the cities and departments in question be liable for millions of dollars in lawsuits.

The theory is that Black life has limited value, and they would rather face the scrutiny than pay the families of the victims. It seems far-fetched if you are not privy to what really happens, but that is the only explanation possible when numerous unbiased witnesses have testified on behalf of the victims and murders are captured on video. This is my opinion—these are my words, and I stand behind them.

Some may think this book was written to criticize and scrutinize the police department. However, as a citizen in the community, I highly value the police department, and I know for a fact that we need them.

In February of 1997, there was no one prouder to be an officer than I was when the LA Police Department stalked and killed the North Hollywood shootout bank robbers. No one admired SWAT Officer Randall Simmons (RIP) the way I did. I have had many exciting moments, but the real reason for sharing my story with the world is to share what happened to me when I tried to do the right thing, and how over twenty years after the fact, I am still running for my life. The torture, harassment, and false accusations are just a few of the things I have experienced over time. I went from feeling blessed to be an officer to being afraid of the police and the system because now I know what they are truly capable of.

I tossed and turned for years, contemplating on how I would tell my story until one day, I woke up from a deep sleep and felt forced to face my fears and write this book. I had a difficult time getting past the thought of bad things that could happen, as well as the reality of facing so many negative experiences head-on. The old me would have breezed through this, as I was totally confident and self-assured that I was the man. Now I have to balance the man I was with the person I have become, who can only see through the eyes of the Post Traumatic Stress Disorder (PTSD) that I now live with. It is a reality that forces me to fight through anxiety, fears, and depression before making a move, let alone writing a book.

Emotional trauma, as well as severe depression, has resulted in the need for medication and a mental hospital stay to cope through anger and bitterness, which are just some of the issues that caused the demise of my marriage. All are a result of my tenure and early retirement as a police officer.

Then there is the physical aspect including but not limited to knee, neck, and back pain, along with going blind and having massive weight gain due to the enormous stress. Like LA, precincts across the United States probably have ex-officers with similar or identical stories. I was not the only one in my department that dealt with unimaginable mistreatment by those in power. Others, such as Christopher Dorner, lost their minds and their lives from the horrific and unjustified treatment inflicted on good police officers.

Most of the time, we were like superheroes, saving women from abusive men, men from provoking women, protecting kids from situations that could have gone bad, ensuring safety rules were followed by the motorist, and even saving lives. When we walked in a room, sat in our police cars to keep watch, or sped to the aid of an accident or tragedy, I felt good…I felt blessed to play such an important role in the community. However, I also witnessed—and surprisingly experienced defamation of character—lying on legal documents, falsified prosecutions, murders, brutality, and bragging about the mistreatment of citizens.

Since swearing to uphold the laws of the land, up until today, I was on the OJ Simpson defense witness crime scene with Mark Furman. In the heart of the LA Riots, I witnessed the death of a childhood friend unjustly killed by fellow officers, witnessed the murder of a fellow officer, had my house shot-up, blackballed by chiefs and an entire sheriff's department, and I was even arrested.

My stories will shock you. However, I accept that through me, the reality of life lessons may seem ridiculous, which is why I choose not to fight back physically but will confront the issues on paper to make a change. Together, we have an opportunity to control our destiny and change our society, but we must start by looking at ourselves.

For those of you who would ask, "Why did it take so long?" I can only explain that for years I wanted to talk about everything, and for years I wanted to get this monkey of pain, hatred, unfairness, and confusion off my back. I guess on this day, after witnessing so many recurring circumstances, God has given me the vision and courage to begin to tell my story.

CHAPTER 1

Growing Up in the Hood

"Deep inside, I have always despised those who commit crimes or bully other people."

My Family

In the early 1960s, my family migrated from Marshall, Texas; The home of Wiley College, a small town in East Texas where the Movie "The Great Debaters" was filmed. My mother and father were both born there. They then moved to Dallas, Texas, had my three sisters, Then moved to Los Angeles where I was born in 1964.

I was the youngest in the family of four children. Having three sisters, with the youngest being five years older than me, I spent much of my childhood years doing things by myself or with friends in the neighborhood. Growing up in Los Angeles near Pico and Normandie, I would certainly have to say our block had its fair share of crime, gangs, poverty, and overall problems that come with being raised in the inner city. I felt lucky to have sisters who were well known for kicking ass. I was not excluded as they also put hands on me to toughen me up. Fighting my sisters made me more confident that I did not have to take any shit in the streets.

My father was a hard-working man who was into construction, gardening, and hunting, while my mother was a part-time stay-at-home mom who would take on odd jobs to help with what we needed financially. They were a true team; if you got in trouble with one, you had to deal with them both.

My Mischievous Side

I was a mild-tempered kid and never looked for trouble, but because of the kids I hung around with, trouble would always seem to find me. Most of my friends were from families who did not have much, so there was always the temptation to be mischievous or commit a crime. I was certainly not raised to be a criminal. nor did I agree with some of the acts. but with peer-pressure, I would at least feel obligated to tag along.

We broke into the local high school and took equipment, and we also stole food to eat from stores. I remember when I was in the sixth grade I took a plastic pencil case from a drug store, and in exchange, my friend was supposed to buy me a Big-Mac meal from McDonald's. Of course, I got caught by the loss prevention officer who then called my mother. Subsequently, I was punished. First, I got a beating from my mother as a warm-up. and when my father got home he whipped my ass too. I never stole again! My first encounter with the police was when I was eight years old. I witnessed a local teenager, who knew my sisters, snatch a purse from an old White lady. He knocked her down, yanked her purse, and ran as fast as he could. The little old lady was on the ground crying and hurt, so I stayed and comforted her until the police arrived. I was very mad at the boy for what he did to the old lady…so mad that I told the police who he was and took them to his house a couple of blocks away. By the look on his face, I could tell that he was mad at me, but due to fear of my sisters, he couldn't do a thing about it. Deep inside, I have always despised those who commit crimes or bully other people.

I had two fights that I can clearly remember. One was when I was in the fifth grade. Somehow, I happened to piss off the kid known as 'The King of the Fifth Grade' because he could whip everybody's ass in a fight. From across the room, he was pounding his fist to gesture that we were going to fight after class. I had a fat knot of anxiety in my stomach… my ass was scared.

Once the bell rang, everyone followed me outside, and once outside, everyone formed a circle around me and 'The King.' He was older, bigger, and tougher than me, and on top of that, he loved to fight. Bravely, I put my fist up in a fighting position, and slowly he started approaching me as I deliberately backed up.

With all the screaming kids yelling, "Get him!" I was able to stall long enough for one of the campus aides to show up and break up the fight before it started. I was happy as hell but had to act like I was disappointed. You can call me lucky because I was surely going to take a whipping that day.

Another fight happened when I was twelve. My friends and I were at the Normandie Recreation Center at Venice Blvd and Normandie, where a bully pushed a kid around who did not want to fight. We were playing touch football at the time, and he was delaying the game, so I asked him to leave the kid alone and let us play ball.

He said, "I'll kick your ass!"

"Boy, I don't have time for you! I don't have to prove anything to you!" I responded immediately.

After that, he rushed me swinging, so I blocked his punches and commenced beating that boy until his face was bloody. He finally gave up, so I stopped thumping him with my fist. After that, he never bothered the other kid or me again.

A Happy Kid

CHAPTER 2

From High School to College

"That was my first opportunity to feel what revenge felt like"

I was four years old in the first grade, thirteen as a freshman at Crenshaw High School, and sixteen when I graduated. When I was fourteen, I made the varsity baseball team with the New York Mets number one draft pick, Darryl Strawberry. However, I never had a chance to play that season because I failed in physical education. I skipped class for two weeks straight to spend time with the first young lady I had ever fallen in love with…Junine Thames. She was cute, friendly, and had a nice smile.

Imagine what it feels like to find out that the girl you secretly admire secretly likes you too. I thought I would spend the rest of my life with her, but after about two weeks, she broke it off with me to go back to her ex-boyfriend. I was crushed, so it took me many years to trust my heart with a girl. Though badly crushed, I somehow got myself together and made it to the varsity baseball team as a senior; however, I quit after the first game. The only true high school accomplishment I can speak of was winning the senior class Friendliest and Most Flirtatious Senior. I made a couple of honor rolls for academic achievement, got my high school diploma, and graduated with my class in 1981.

After high school, like most young men, I was trying to figure out my life. I went to a couple of local junior colleges and worked summers with my father's company, HCB Contractors. One summer, I fell twenty-two feet from the helicopter port to the floor below while pouring cement. I saw my life flash before my eyes as I was falling, thinking it was the end. However, once I realized I was not dead, I knew construction was not for me.

Forced to Grow Up

And time flew to the summer of 1983; I was having a blast being a typical teenager until the unexpected happened—I got a young lady pregnant and suddenly became a teenage father to my daughter, Jonae Jones. Having a baby made me wake up and think like a man. My baby girl forced me to figure out what I wanted to be in life.

At first, I wanted to be a fireman, but the fall at the construction site caused me to be afraid of heights. I knew baseball was what I was best at, but I had not participated in an official season since I was fourteen. I didn't compete in my junior or senior years in high school, so it had been practically three years since I played. However, at eighteen years old, I knew I was stronger, taller, and faster, and since baseball was the only thing I ever loved and was good at, I dove right in and started working out. I went to the batting cages, started jogging, lifted weights, and began to ask around for the leagues to play in. I was all about baseball at that point and worked out for about three weeks before I found a league to play in.

My cousin, Delon Small, and I ended up on a team called the Travelers at the Jackie Robinson Stadium in Compton. It was amazing that I had not played in years, and suddenly I was doing what I loved. I truly felt God had put me on the path to what He wanted me to do. That summer, I was one of the league's best players. It was like riding a bike. I made the all-star teams, which resulted in the professional scouts checking me out.

Michael Strawberry, Darryl Strawberry's big brother, was a family friend and the umpire at most of the games. Michael later became a police officer and a driver for Police Chief Darryl Gates. He would talk to me as I was playing and would smile proudly while I was doing well on the field. Eventually, just knowing him gave me the belief that later in life, I could be an officer too if I wanted to. He was the only cop I knew. Soon the summer ended, and I had risen to be one of the best eighteen-year-old baseball players in the area.

Then there was my coach, Dennis Cole, for the Travelers, who was the brother of linebacker, Robin Cole, for the World

Champion Pittsburg Steelers in the 70s & 80s. Dennis told me about a school I could go to that would be a good place to play ball away from home. He drove me to Palomar College in San Marcos, California…a quiet place thirty-five miles west of San Diego. He connected me with the baseball coach, and I got an apartment with three other guys from LA, where I stayed for one month. Since baseball had not yet started, I often went to the gym to lift weights and play basketball to stay in shape. After watching me play, the basketball coach asked me to try out for his team. Coming from Crenshaw High, a known powerhouse in basketball, I was decent, but I was nothing like my real "Shaw" ballers. I ended up playing both baseball and basketball for a while.

One day, the football coach saw me catching passes with my roommates who were on the football team, and he asked me to play football as well. I ended up with too many distractions and lost focus. When it was all said and done, I got cut from the baseball team because I missed way too many practices. I then quit the basketball team, checked out of Palomar Junior College, and transferred to San Diego City College.

I moved in with my cousin Lafayette Carter, who was already attending San Diego State University; he is now a Fire Captain for the Los Angeles Fire Department (LAFD). The harmony between us was great. Following his lead of being focused, I became disciplined in the classroom and in baseball. Although we were focused, we partied our asses off!

In baseball, I made the first team all-conference, which ironically was in the same league as Palomar College...the team that cut me. That was my first opportunity to understand what revenge felt like. I performed at an extremely high level against them – I killed that team every time! It felt good... real good! I was so talented that I ended up getting drafted by the St. Louis Cardinals professional baseball team.

After leaving San Diego City College, I ended up declining to sign the contract with the Cardinals because they wanted me to go to a college in Texas and play first. I decided to go back home so that I could help with my daughter and attend Cal State Dominquez Hills in Carson. There, my coach was the infamous Andy Lopez, winner of the national championships at Pepperdine University, University of Florida, and the University of Arizona. He took our team at Cal State to the Division Two College World Series before moving on to the prime Division One colleges and having an exceptional career.

My first year, after having one of the top batting averages on the team in the fall season, I ended up not playing nearly as much as I wanted to when the regular season began. Like most young guys who do not get their way, I blamed the coach and accused him of being prejudiced, when in reality, we had an All-American in the left field and an All-American in the right field.

I was not a good outfielder defensively as I had just started playing outfield two years prior. My time on the field was not about race at all; I was simply in a highly competitive situation with athletes that were better than me. Lord knows I could not accept that, and I didn't realize the value of my position at the time. I was the pinch hitter, which was the designated hitter when we were in a crunch and needed someone to bring in the win.

When we played in the World Series, I made all-West Region, and by my senior year in 1987-1988, I was in the starting lineup of every game. I learned that "nothing is given to you…you have to earn your opportunities in life."

My Senior Year at Crenshaw High

Pulled Over

Things didn't always go smoothly when I was in college, as run-ins with the law were inevitable if you were Black or Brown. I remember while in college in my junior year, two of my Hispanic teammates and I had an encounter with the police. We went to work out at a fitness center in Torrance; when we were done and exiting the parking lot, the Torrance police pulled us over, causing us to be nervous because there was a gun in the car. We were all like, "What the hell!" The Torrance Police Department had a reputation for being aggressive with minorities. We were not gang bangers; we were all top-notch college athletes with no criminal records.

When the officers got out of their car, we were shaking as they demanded, "License and registration please!"

Then one of them said, "Do you know why we stopped you?"

"No officer!"

"You made a left turn from the parking lot. It says no left turn."

"Sir, we apologize. We never saw that sign," I responded.

"Where are you coming from?"

"Sir, we're coming from the fitness center. We are baseball players at CSUDH."

He said, "Really? Okay, I'm going to just give you a warning this time. Just be aware from now on." He preceded to give back the license and registration and let us go.

We were happy as hell as we thought for sure we were going to jail. The funny thing was, all three of us later became cops in different areas of Southern California, and one of us ended up working for the Torrance Police Department.

My Chance for the Pros

Once the semester ended, I played and was a team leader for the Chicago White Sox pro summer league. I was hitting exceptionally well and also started pitching, which was something I knew I could do but had never tried. I did not realize how effective I was as a pitcher until my last game at Cerritos College. All the professional baseball scouts, who needed to sign a player, were at the game to see me play. I knew I would play both positions – batter and pitcher – that game, so I mistakenly warmed up as a pitcher for ten minutes in the bullpen. I then went into the outfield for pre-game infield and outfield warm-ups, which I had never done before.

I was in right-field, approaching the ball hit by the coach for my first throw to third base. I put my glove down, caught the ground ball, lifted my arm so I could make a strong throw to show off my speed, accuracy, and strength to the scouts. Immediately when I threw the ball, I felt a pop and excruciating pain in my elbow. My tendon had popped away from the bone, and my arm was hanging. I was done! My chance of ever being a professional baseball player was over… It was a heartbreaking moment.

I immediately ran back to the dugout, crying while holding my arm. The tears were due to both the pain and the reality that I would never play again. What was even worse was that when I looked up, I noticed two of the four scouts leaving.

I did not have medical insurance, so I had to wait until Monday to see my trainer at school. After that, my dad helped me get on a full-time roster at an HCB Construction company as an engineer, where I worked with an injured arm. Because I was a new father, I wanted stability, a good salary, and benefits to take care of my daughter, so I took the test and started the process to become a police officer.

San Diego City College, St Louis Cardinals
Draft Choice & CSUDH

Office Engineer at HCB Contractors

CHAPTER 3

The Academy

"I went from being the best athlete and motivated officer to a man in a downward spiral of an entire career."

The Academy brought many challenges, and every day was different. However, I was so confident about my destiny to be an officer that I knew I would not fail. I was strong, smart, and had great common sense with the belief I could help save the world. Combined all of that with growing up in a tough neighborhood around Hispanic and Black gang bangers, conmen, dope dealers, bullies, and everything else in the hood...I was ready.

Training included learning investigative techniques, state laws, computer literacy, and reporting to manage the administrative duties associated with the job. We also learned fighting techniques, how to subdue suspects, use our weapons, rules of engagement, and first aid. We were ready to handle multiple situations in the city, but what we were never prepared for was how to deal with real-life scenarios when witnessing criminal activity within the police force.

Two months prior to finishing the police academy, I experienced my first ride-along at the Wilshire Division. At that point, I was proud that I was going to be a respected cop. Our entire class was sent to various divisions to do regular police work with only four months of training. We were scheduled to work the tough shifts and do real police work in the midst of street violence to see if we could hang. I worked with those who were known to be "Real Gun Slingers!"

I remember working with Officer Smith, a rugged, beach-boy-looking White cop who carried two large handguns on his waist. My first impression of him was that he was sharp and all about police work. I was a rookie, so I was the passenger simply keeping the books and following my partner's lead.

We were patrolling late at night in a dangerous area, known to be the Marvin Avenue gang neighborhood in the Wilshire division. We stopped in front of a rough-looking apartment building, and after we looked around the front, he drove around the corner to the complex immediately behind the building and parked. I had no clue what he was looking for, and I did not ask questions…I naturally followed.

Officer Smith got out of the car, so I got out. He proceeded to jump over the fence leading to the apartments, so I followed. He pulled his weapon out and began walking in a search position with his gun pointed in front of him, so I did too. Suddenly, I could hear loud music, and when we turned the corner, we unexpectedly ended up in the center courtyard of the building. There were around twenty-five to thirty Marvin Ave gangsters all around and above us.

My partner pointed his gun at them and yelled out commands…"Get your Hands up and don't Move!"

So once again, I did exactly what my training officer did. The truth is, I was nervous as hell as there was no way we could keep our eyes on all of them.

The Crips kept yelling back at us. "What the fuck we do, Cuzz? Why y'all fucking with us?"

As my partner was yelling commands, he also requested back-up and an air-unit. Before I knew it, the lights from the helicopter were shining down on us, and additional units were there to back us up.

That was only my second encounter as an officer, and I was happy as hell to see the back-up officers. All we ended up doing was checking everyone's identification, and then we let them all go. To this day, I wondered why we risked our lives by sneaking up on them when a crime was not being committed. I also wondered if my partner was caught off-guard like I was with it being two of us and so many of them—no harm, no foul, though.

Dealing with so many gangsters at once gave me even more confidence to finish at the academy and graduate. Lo and behold, as I was finishing my last month in the academy, I accidentally fell on an obstacle course. My injury was so bad that I had to have surgery and was told that I would never be able to work in the field again.

Physically Fit

Under normal circumstances, an officer's probation period is one year. However, my efforts to step up my game may have cost me. I finished strong academically and with minimal misses when shooting targets. I was so driven that 1 began to work out and run even at home on weekends so I could become the best officer I could be. I had already passed my first two physical exams, so I knew I would graduate. What they had not seen was a Joe Jones that was motivated and inspired. I was just going through the motions.

My two best friends and the best athletes in academy class 3-89 were Marvin Brent, our class leader, and Eric Moore, LA Police Department Hall of Fame basketball player. Although we hung together tough and played basketball against each other in class, we also partied together. Yes, police recruits partied! Although I had been at college and was drafted to be a professional baseball player, training as an officer caused me to be in the best shape of my life.

The final PFQ (Physical Fitness Qualifier) consisted of several physical exams back to back, a dummy drag, and an obstacle course. It was my turn, and I myself was amazed at how calm I was; I believe it was so because I was indeed prepared. Once the starting gun went off, I breezed through the first part of the exam. During the obstacle course, I was flying through with the mindset of breaking the record for the time. At the last and most difficult part of the course, the seventh wall, I allowed my confidence to get the best of me.

As opposed to going over the wall headfirst, my ass thought I could fly! I literally jumped up with my hands first, and in the same motion, I tried to bring my feet over the six-foot wall in one motion. The problem was that I did not lift my feet high enough, so they clipped the wall, and I flipped over head-first.

The force caused me to jam my feet to the ground with extreme force. The pain was so bad that I thought I had broken both feet. The doctor said I would have been better off if I had broken a bone as opposed to the type of trauma my feet experienced. Unfortunately, I finished the rest of the academy on crutches. I had to have surgery on my left big toe, which affected my entire equilibrium. I went from being the best athlete and most motivated officer to a man in a downward spiral of an entire career. It took a while for me to realize it, but I was no longer my normal self.

I could not walk, run, or do anything without pain. Since I was injured right out of the academy, I completed my first six months working light duty at the desk of the West Valley Division. I was told I would probably never be able to work patrol due to the seriousness of the pain in my foot. The thought of working the desk for my entire career or having to leave my job altogether really made me upset.

Determination

While going through physical therapy and rehab, I started to get depressed. I kept trying to figure out how I would become healthy again. The fact that I could not run made me lazy and almost crazy. So one day, I decided that on my day off, I would finally move around and go to the park in Woodland Hills. Although my foot was sore, I decided to play pick-up basketball to get my heart rate up. The moment I started playing, my toe started throbbing, but I kept pushing myself; my intent was to exercise and feel better about myself.

We played five on five, and the other team happened to have two guys that proceeded to antagonize my teammates. I thought to myself, "We're way out here in the valley, and dudes act like this?"

One of them said, "None of you motherfuckers better not foul me, or it's on. I just got out and felt like fucking somebody up anyway!" He had a homeboy with him that went along with everything he said.

Somehow, a kid on my team and I developed a connection in the short period of playing together when suddenly one of the troublemakers began picking a fight with the kid.

I said, "Come on, fellas, I'm out here just trying to get some exercise!"

One of the guys responded, "Shut up! I'll whip yo ass!"

I said to myself, "Damn! Here we go!"

I did not respond; I just kept playing. The next time down the court, we were under the basket about to go for a rebound when, all of a sudden, one of the guys from the other team hit me in the stomach with an elbow, knocking the wind out of me.

I bent down against the fence to give myself a moment to catch my breath. Once I caught my breath, I came off the fence and punched the asshole in his face…and the fight was on.

I continued to follow up with my punches as his friend came from behind and hit me in the back of the head with his fist. Before I knew it, they were both coming at me at the same time. All I remember was swinging my ass off, landing punches while barely being hit.

Suddenly, the kid I connected with picked up a Gatorade bottle while screaming, "Leave him alone!" He threw the bottle aiming for the head of one of the guys. If that dude had not ducked, the boy would have busted his face open.

At that point, one of the guys started running toward the parking lot as if he was heading to the car to get a gun. I also headed to my car to get my gun out of the trunk, just in case. Suddenly, I noticed that the kid had disappeared, so I got my gun out of the trunk, got in my car, and hurried toward the exit.

We never called the police for that type of shit. You fight and live to see another day. I wanted to thank the kid for being brave and helping me out, but I never saw him again.

After the park brawl, I said to myself, "Well, I can still fight! There has to be a way I can still get back on patrol."

So, I spoke to my doctor and asked if there was a shoe that I could wear that would hold my toe in one place, not allowing it to bend. He decided that he would create an orthotic shoe with a steel plate and an arch to the sole of my left shoe.

Once the shoes were complete, I wore them for a few days, and the pain was poof. Soon, I requested, with my doctor's permission, to be granted the ability to continue my probationary period as a patrol officer. Though I was given the approval, it extended my probation by another six months.

CHAPTER 4

On the Job Training

"How would you like it if someone jacked your family up for no reason? What you said was disrespectful!"

I will never forget my first day working as a day watch patrol in the West Valley Division (WVAL). We reported to roll call where the Watch Commander was giving assignments, reading crime information, and giving insight on what to look for and focus on. I remember him calling out a robbery and vehicle description that involved Black males on Ventura Blvd. The Watch Commander clearly stated, "Be sure to focus on the description of the car and make stops of vehicles that fit the description."

Suddenly, a tall White officer in the front of the room said with total confidence and aggression, "Forget that! Let's just jack all of their asses up like we did in the old days!" Other officers and the Watch Commander chimed in as well as if the profiling was a joke. I do not recall what was said by the officers as I was too pissed by what the first one said. After the roll call ended, I was to get the shotgun and radios from the kit room and find out who my training officer would be. Guess who it was? The same tall, White officer who had just had a case of racist diarrhea in roll call.

"Meet me at the car, and I'll prep you on preparing the car," he said. He was not aware that I was already trained to prep the squad car and could do it with my eyes closed. When he got to the cruiser, he was amazed that I had already entered all information on the log, loaded the shotgun, searched the vehicle, and logged in on the Mobile Data Terminal (MDT), the communication monitor in the police car.

He got in on the driver's side, checked everything, and said, "Good Job!" I didn't say a word in response as I was still stuck on his previous comment.

We pulled out of the lot and drove a mile away from the station in complete silence for some time. Finally, he said, "I guess you had a problem with what I said in roll call?"

I looked up at him with a serious face and said, "You damn right. I did!" The truth is, I do not know if he knew I was in roll call at the time that he made the comment. I was the only Black working day watch at the time, and I was in the back of the room. However, it did not matter to me. I repeated, "I definitely had a problem with what you said!" There was silence, and then I went on to say, "How would you like it if someone jacked your family up for no reason? What you said was disrespectful!"

He proceeded to pull the car over and explained his thoughts. As he began to ramble, I heard him talking, but I didn't – I knew he was just trying to cover his ass. Either way, I believe he got the point that I was not putting up with racist bullshit, and I would speak my mind. He must have gotten something from the exchange because he showed me a great deal of respect for the next two months while I was his probationer. I made sure to be at my best as I knew his mentality. My ratings were good, and he treated me fairly. We got past what I thought was going to be an ugly situation.

The Chase

I worked at night with my second probation officer, John; he was also very well, a tall White officer. Right off the bat, he allowed my work to dictate how he treated me. What he liked about me was the fact that I listened to and took initiative. He was absolutely a no-nonsense police officer; he taught me as much as any officer had taught me in my entire career.

We wrote tickets, looked for dope, participated in high-speed chases, and I experienced my first use of force incident. Like it was yesterday, I remember when we were patrolling in the Canoga Park area of WVAL, we saw a dark-colored car run the light at Sherman Way and Canoga. We followed the car since the driver was overspeeding. As we caught up, he started going faster. We put on our lights and siren, but he would not stop.

We announced over the radio that we were in pursuit of a vehicle with the description and direction of where we were headed. As we were in pursuit, his car went out of control and crashed into a tree about a mile from where we started. The suspect, a White male about six feet with a white t-shirt on, jumped out of the car and started running.

My partner slowed down to let me out, and I started chasing him on foot. He ran for a block before I caught up with him and dove on his back, tackling him to the ground. He tried to roll over and swing at me, so I punched him in the face a couple of times and tried to grab his arms.

By then, Officer John jumped out of the car and started hitting the suspect with his baton. Soon, blood was everywhere, but the crazy dude was still fighting. At some point, he quit resisting; we cuffed him and took him into custody. After running the vehicle, we found that it was stolen. We had the fire department treat him for his injuries and booked him for grand theft auto. Luckily, I did not get hurt, and John also appreciated my effort. However, he said, "With my help, of course!" That was the moment where we shared our first laugh.

Same but Different

We shared many moments that contributed to our growing bond. John would take me to places where he liked to eat, and he had relationships with restaurants that gave officers free food. However, he loved to eat at In & Out Burger whenever we started our shift. I think he also liked the fact that I was a former baseball player. I had professional baseball player friends that lived in the division, and as I became comfortable with him, I would let him meet them.

Darryl Strawberry, Chris Brown (RIP), and Eric Davis were all living in the area, and he met them all. However, he paid back the favor by hooking me up with my tax lady, Joan, an older lady that was sweet as all outdoors. "She ain't nothing pretty to look at, but she'll get you some money at the end of the year!" That woman knew her taxes, and she hooked me up every year. I ended up using her services until she died some eight or nine years later.

One night we got a call of an active burglary in progress. When we got to the house, we parked a block away and approached on foot. Once at the house, I searched the front, and my partner searched the back. After searching for a few minutes, we determined it was a C-4, meaning that the suspects were no longer there. I knocked on the front door while announcing our presence at the same time.

"Police!" I saw a Caucasian lady look out the window. "Come open the door," I told her.

Keep in mind that I was in full uniform with a shiny badge on my chest, but she would not open the door. I decided to call my White partner to summon her to open the door. When he knocked, she came back to the door, and when she saw him, she opened the door.

I thought to myself, "What the fuck is her issue?"

That let me know that even as an officer, I am stereotyped, mistreated, and disrespected as a Black man.

MLB Baseball Stars Eric Davis, Daryl Strawberry & Me

The Bully

As time went on, I began to work as Police Officer-2 since I completed most of the sign-offs in my probation book. One officer was Big Mike, a huge Jewish officer who stood about 6'5" with big ass arms, a mean face, and what many believed to be a crazy mentality. The truth was that most of the officers feared "Big Mike." I guess if I were looking for a fight, he would not be where I would start.

I remember the first day we worked together. When he realized he was working with me, he told me to get the car ready. I guess the line to get a car was slightly slower that day because I was not ready when he thought I should be.

While we were still in the station and in front of the other officers, he yelled, "Boot," at me, which means officer on probation. "You ain't got the fucking car yet?" A couple of the other officers laughed while I was slightly pissed from the disrespect, so I did not respond.

At the same time, I was handed the keys and shotgun, he yelled again. "Boot, what's up with the car?"

I walked about twenty feet to where he was, and in front of the same laughing officers, I looked him straight in his eyes and said, "Who in the fuck you think you talking to?"

With his naturally angry-looking face, he said, "Man, I was just checking! I'll meet you at the car." We met up at the vehicle, prepped it to go on patrol, and that was our formal introduction.

From that moment forward, we were cool. He had the other officers in line, but I was used to bullies and was not about to let a White officer disrespect me or put fear in my heart. Some would think that a young Black male would have many issues working in a ninety-eight percent White police station in the early nineties, but the WVAL Division was not bad at all compared to the things I was about to experience.

I had a few conflicting situations while working there, but I could confidently say that if I had stayed in the valley as an officer, I would have enjoyed a long successful career.

The Badge

You go through the process of becoming a police officer without knowing what to expect...testing, physicals, mental evaluations, background checks, and many other ways to find out if you're cut out to be hated by people from all walks of life. People of all ages and colors despise the law enforcers with a badge besides scared people, who need the cops on a regular basis, or Whites in upscale or suburban areas, who have no idea what it feels like to get jacked up by the police; they are the same people who can argue with the cops and tell them, "I pay your salary!"

Then, of course, there were many single females of different nationalities looking for a man with benefits to provide them and their baby with stability. Their line was, "I love a man in a uniform!" At the very least, they knew they would have a man that could not physically abuse them without serious backlash.

The other awkward relationship was with Black people, including family and friends. My own people looked at me differently and made a point to let everyone know that I was a cop. When I would walk into a room at a family gathering, my own family would start whispering or discontinue their conversations, which made me feel awkward. If only they knew I could care less about what they did. When I was home,

I was at home trying to absorb normalcy, doing all I could to get away from the backstabbing and the uncomfortable feeling of being around people on the job. I have no idea how things translate in White, Hispanic, or Asian families, but in Black families, when you become a police officer, things are different.

At the time I became an officer, not one person in my family had ever been in law enforcement. I had no officer lineage and no experiences to draw from. I wanted to be the one who made a difference. All I knew about it were the multiple times I had been pulled over by the police and cited or the many experiences I heard about from people I loved. It wasn't often, but here and there, I heard of people getting off with a warning.

My family is my family. We come from the same place. None of them were familiar with the police, and now they have a family member who was on the same side as those who have arrested, abused, and instilled fear in their hearts for years. How could it truly even be all about me? All they can recall is how vulnerable the police made them feel at times. This is how deep it is. Once you cross that line, even as family, they simply don't know what to feel. So, when you come around family...it is what it is.

Things Changed

The first two friends that let me know my life would no longer be the same were brothers that lived two-hundred feet away from my house. Unfortunately, I will not be able to reveal their names, just know they were childhood friends with extremely strict parents.

Although we grew up together, they chose the streets as opposed to the scholarly life their parents had set up for them. If you had to guess, even I would have said that the street life was a more possible outcome for me than for them. Not because I was a bad kid, it is just that they were church-going bookworms with a very structured upbringing, and they both played varsity basketball.

Fast forward eight years, things changed for all of us. The brothers moved out of the old neighborhood, and I moved with my mom after my parents divorced. Even with us living far apart, we remained friends, so I used to go to their house on 3rd Ave near 39th Street in South Central Los Angeles. The time period was known as the Roaring 80s, and the dope game was at its peak. They lived directly across the street from one of the high rollers in the hood, and we would just sit and watch the dope game from a distance. We would lift weights and talk about our dreams as we looked across the street at Porsches, Mercedes, and all kinds of other flashy cars with nice rims, visiting the house daily.

Around the same time that I started the process to become a police officer, a traumatic situation occurred that I would never forget. I went to drop something off to the brothers before they went to work. This time, things seemed vastly different because all the flashy cars were still parked in front of the house across the street. Typically, the only cars that were there were those of the people who lived there.

I said to myself, "That is extremely odd."

When I got home that evening, to my surprise, there was a tragedy. I happened to be watching TV and a news flash posted with tow-trucks pulling several fancy cars away from a house. I immediately thought that the home looked like the cars I saw that morning. It turned out that the incident was across the street from my friends.

According to the news report, about six people were executed in the house during a robbery, and the murders were discovered after a baby was seen crawling in front of the house. When they went into the home, the bodies were discovered. Several well-known dope dealers and a couple of females were killed. That was a big deal in the community. Things were bad!

I joined the police force, and the brothers went on to do something different with their lives. I had graduated from the police academy, and the brothers had become dope dealers. Two humble kids I knew growing up succumbed to the pressure of money. I guess living so close to drug dealers for years and watching the money that was made became an irresistible temptation for them. The gangs, drugs, and other pressures were the very reason my father wanted me out of LA to go to college in San Diego. I could have easily fallen into the same temptations.

Our friendship ended due to my profession, and they never called me again. If I bumped into them on the street, they would always have excuses as to why they did not call, but I knew exactly why they pulled away. We never really saw each other much after that until about ten years later.

After I left the force, I saw one of them parked across the street at Hancock Park, talking to someone I did not know. He went to his trunk and removed a package, and the guy handed him an envelope. They made this exchange around twenty feet from my front door. He did not know I lived there and that I had eyes on him the whole time.

CHAPTER 5

Black is Black | CJ-Mac

*"White People and the affluent appear to have a
separate justice system."*

CJ Mac

Bryaan Ross, aka CJ Mac, and I grew up about five
blocks from one another, which were rival blocks in our
neighborhood. Many of us attended Mt. Vernon Junior High
with the Black gangs, and others attended Berendo Junior
High, where the Mexican gang ruled. We were the same age,
but for some unknown reason, he thought that he was tougher
than me, and our mutual friend, Grady Williams, used to
brag about how good of a fighter he was. I was a leader on
my block, so I didn't fear or care about what Bryaan could do.

One day, Grady challenged our block to a football game.
My homeboys and I were like, "Hell yea! Let's do it!"

We met up on a Saturday morning a few days later, at
15th and Harvard Blvd. It was a nice day with perfect weather
to whip their ass, but as soon as the game started, I could

see that they were better than I thought. Bryaan felt it was necessary to guard me, and while doing so, he tried to punk me. He was looking me up and down, was extremely physical, and at one point, he got in my face like he wanted to fight.

"Cuz, I'll fuck you up!" he said. Still, I was not backing down and stood toe to toe with him until they broke us up.

We didn't end up fighting, but it was a very competitive and close game. I don't remember who won, but I know that although we all gained mutual respect, I didn't like Bryaan, and the feeling was mutual. He thought he was hard because of his family ties to the Rolling 60 Crips.

After junior high, Bryaan went to LA High, and I went to Crenshaw High. Several years later, we ran into each other, and that is when I found out that Bryaan was the cousin of one of the baseball players at Crenshaw that my family and I knew very well. That discussion alone seemed to take the edge off our dislike for each other. However, by that time, Bryaan was gang banging and doing street shit while I was trying to stay focused in school and sports. I graduated from high school and went on to college to play ball while Bryaan was a menace to society, bouncing in and out of jail.

Bryaan was rehabilitated from being in and out of jail, and subsequently, that's when he became known as Rapper CJ Mac. One evening, about five years later, I was on routine patrol as an officer in the Wilshire area, and I saw Bryaan driving down the street. I put my lights on and pulled him over. He could not see me as I approached. In a rude and disrespectful tone in my voice, I said, "Where the fuck are you going, homeboy?"

I could tell he was agitated and angry for being stopped by the police. He said, "What's the problem?"

"Your ass is going to jail! That's the problem!" Then without him seeing me, I walked all the way up to the window laughing my ass off and said, "Got you!"

He turned and saw it was me, and you could see the relief on his face. He said, "Mannnnn! What the fuck! I thought I was done!" He got out of the car, and we embraced, shook hands, and laughed. That is when we officially became cool with each other.

CJ Mac went on to have a respected music career, and I continued working as a police officer for a few more years. He would always tell people in the streets that I was a cop he truly respected because he knew first-hand that I had heart. I guess he felt that way because I never backed down from him when we were kids and because he and his family know and respect me.

Since then, we reconnected as I was coaching my sons at the Crenshaw YMCA and his son played as well. Knowing where he came from, I was impressed that he became an involved parent and was participating in his son's sporting events. We spoke enough to be cordial with each other, and I even attended one of his music video shoots on Crenshaw Boulevard. His music was good. I knew he rapped about things he experienced and was signed by the same crew that Ice-Cube was involved with.

Black is Black

Now, some twenty years later, we are both grown men who successfully raised our children. Bryaan Ross, aka CJ Mac, is now a published author and businessman who turned out to be a quality human being with a mission to rehabilitate gang members. So many are locked up for long and extended sentences with the Three Strikes law. The strategic and systemic unfair sentencing measures targeted to keep Black men in jail for cheap labor is also a ploy to weaken the Black family by taking the men from their homes and preventing them from raising their children. Sadly, sentencing in many circumstances is not fair.

White people and the affluent appear to have a separate justice system while Black men consistently deal with racial injustice, being treated more harshly because of the color of their skin. Fortunately, Bryaan was given a chance. Then you have me…a man who was prepared to protect and serve citizens. I loved helping people, doing honest police work, and being a part of a team.

I was ready to be a career officer but found out that the same inequity, prejudice, and politics that vex our Black men on the streets, encaging them for life, can also ruin the career and family of a law-abiding officer. Bryaan and I are two Black men who took totally different routes in life but somehow experienced the same atrocities of being Black in America. As a gang member or a cop, Black is Black. I thank God we are both still here to tell our stories.

CHAPTER 6

Intent to Kill

"My wife and I hugged as if to be relieved and surprised we were still alive. She began to cry, saying, 'Who would do this?' I held her and said, 'Baby, I don't know'."

Not long after getting the authorization to go in the field, I was blown away with bad news. On March 4, 1990, my good friend and mentee, Hank Gathers (LMU Basketball Star), who I loved and had great respect for, died of a heart problem during a basketball game. There were three of us that stayed together…me, my best friend Robert Cannon of the Los Angeles Fire Department, and Hank, who at the time was Robert's roommate – we all grew to be close friends. Although he was the best basketball player in the nation at the time, Hank liked me because I was not one to kiss his ass. I was always looking for ways for him to improve his game, and he appreciated that since he wanted to be the best. I attended and cheered him on at every single game except for the last game, where the giant fell to his death. As hard as I tried, I could not get off work that day to watch him play.

The most important spawning was my lifelong friendship with LMU point guard Terrell Lowery, who Hank mentored and took to me after his passing, and as well I married my childhood friend and longtime girlfriend, Cynthia Jones. My now ex-wife, Cynthia Jones, and I met in the sixth grade. Even at that time, I knew she was a keeper. Initially, I had a fear of commitment, but when Hank died, I quickly realized that life was way too short, so I got married three weeks after he passed away. After getting married, I moved from my apartment in the Valley to a home I purchased in the heart of Los Angeles. That house would later be the scene of what could have ended as a tragedy.

I do not know what led to the incident that made that night a living hell for my wife and me, but it was a moment that, although I have my theories, is still a mystery today. We were both at home after work, had just finished eating dinner, and decided to head to the bedroom. It was around 9:00 pm, so I am not sure why I left the kitchen light on, but my unintentional action probably saved our lives. Around ten seconds after we walked into the bedroom, we suddenly heard gunshots, the shattering of breaking glass, and the ricocheting of wood from the bullets that sprayed into our home.

I immediately pulled my pregnant wife to the floor and grabbed my service revolver for protection. The shots were so loud and vicious that it felt like we were in a war zone and that my wife and I were the targets.

BOOM! BOOM! BANG!

The shattering of glass over and over seemed to go on forever. While ducking, I was able to call the police, let them know that I was an off-duty police officer and that my house was being shot up.

"Get here, 911!" I said with extreme urgency.

My wife was hysterically crying, and I tried to console her while paying attention to our surroundings, with my gun pointed back and forth from the door to the windows, ready to shoot at whoever was trying to kill us.

We stayed in the bedroom, and after about two minutes, the shooting stopped. I kept my wife down and made sure she stayed silent so I could hear if anyone approached us. Soon, I heard a helicopter, and immediately after that, I saw flashlights and heard the police. The officers ordered us to come out with our hands where they could see them. I slowly opened the door, and we exited the bedroom, leaving my gun in the room to avoid a misunderstanding. As we walked through the house, the evidence of an intent to kill was apparent. The kitchen looked like a war zone with plaster, broken glass, wood chips, and holes everywhere.

My wife and I hugged as if to be relieved and surprised that we were still alive. She began to cry, saying, "Who would do this?"

I held her and said, "Baby, I don't know."

The police then took us outside as they went through our house with a fine- tooth comb for evidence. It was by far the worst thing I had ever experienced in my life up until that point, and we were never the same. I really wanted to believe that this was a case of the perpetrators hitting the wrong house, but my inflated fears were not something I could just simply forget. My house was riddled with bullets from a thirty-eight, a nine-millimeter, and a shotgun: all weapons authorized and used by the police department.

Major Crimes handled the investigation, and it was revealed that two to three gunmen stood outside my gate and shot into the kitchen. At the time, there were no known suspects or leads. Luckily, my gate was stuck and made noise, so they did not go in the backyard where they would have heard exactly where we were in the house.

When thinking back on who would try to kill us, all I could remember was the disagreement that I had earlier with a sergeant. He appeared to be angry with me because I was working an off-duty job without a permit, and the same sergeant was working the investigation at my house. The unnecessary debate with him was the only thing I could think of at the time, so I brushed it off, believing that we were not the intended mark.

At that point, it felt as if our lives were a mess! We were scared and knew someone was trying to kill us. But who? We went to stay with my mother-in-law as the Metropolitan police division officers secured our house. They also followed us everywhere we went in the vicinity of our home and provided me with a take-home rover so that I had direct contact with the police in case of an emergency. I was thankful and felt good that the department expressed concern for me and my wife's safety. Although worried, I felt like the police department had my back until a couple of days after the shooting; while officers were sitting in the driveway of my house, two people were murdered, two houses down from my home. That heightened our fear, especially since the killers got away.

We had to stay with my mother-in-law, and I was still in fear from continuously watching my back, so things were chaotic. The court liaison did not have my pager number; as a result, he was unable to reach me to let me know that I needed to show up to court for a case that went to trial. Even though the missed appearance was not my fault, my captain punished me with two days off without pay.

This was devastating to me. I did not understand how they could be so insensitive. This was the first of many questionable moves by the police department.

CHAPTER 7

Trouble Always Found Me

"I noticed he was holding his throat with blood oozing through his hands saying, 'This guy is robbing me!'"

The shooting and the stress that I was experiencing as an officer triggered problems in my marriage, causing my wife and me to seek professional help. We were headed northbound on Broadway Blvd approaching the 101 Freeway when I looked to my right and saw something that did not seem right. A Hispanic man stood on the opposite side of the guardrail on the overpass, appearing as if he were about to jump. I also noticed that there was an older man talking to him, appearing to try and convince him not to take his own life. Immediately, I pulled my car to the right and told my wife to call 911 to let them know about the jumper.

As I got closer, it was exactly as I thought. The older man was around sixty-five, five feet tall, and had a thin build. He said, "No, don't do that!" The man, who stood about five feet, eleven inches, and appeared to be over two hundred pounds, was planning to jump to his death. He seemed very agitated and upset about something that happened in his life. He looked down, anticipating his jump.

I was about two feet away, slowly easing on them, and said, "My friend, don't do this! Everything is going to be OK. Let's talk about it."

Suddenly, I reached over past the old man and grabbed the suicidal guy as he pushed off the ledge to jump. I held onto the old man to keep him from being pulled over the rail while also holding the young man who was dangling by his feet, determined to end his life.

He was yelling, "No! No!"

I pulled and struggled, dragging him over the rail to safety. In his attempt to complete his mission, the man started crying and swinging at me, so I put him in a hold down on the ground and held him there until the police arrived.

As the police unit showed up, they approached while clapping their hands and telling me that what I did was brave. After the police handcuffed him, I commended the old man, letting him know that he was a good person for trying to help. When the officers asked what happened, I identified myself as an off- duty police officer and explained that we just happened to be driving by when I noticed the man looking as if he was going to commit suicide.

A sergeant from Central Division showed up and asked for my division and my statement. After sharing details with the officers about the incident, my wife and I proceeded to our appointment. A few weeks later, while passing in the hallway, a Wilshire Division Sergeant, Greg Montgomery, presented me with a commendation that looked like it had been sitting around for a while.

I thought to myself, "I risked my own life while saving two lives, and this is how you recognize my efforts?"

Just "Here's your copy Jones, sign this." I didn't do it for police credit; I just wondered if I were White and one of their favorites, would it have been handled the same way? I witnessed officers getting a medal of valor for less.

A Big Heart

My heroic deeds started before I ever considered being an officer. I always had a big heart and did my best to help people whenever I could. I remember a few situations occurring right in front of me, and some of them did not turn out as I had hoped.

In January of 1989, while still in the Academy and serving my month ride- along, I was off-duty and on my way to Wilshire Station to work my shift. The situation that happened left me second-guessing myself when it came to my career choice. I was driving northbound on Buckingham from Jefferson Blvd, and as I approached 29th St., I saw a taxi heading southbound, veer to the right, and run over a fire hydrant, causing water to shoot thirty feet high into the sky. I heard the driver yell, and at the same time, I noticed he was holding his throat with blood oozing through his hands. He said, "This guy is robbing me."

Suddenly, a large Black man emerged from the back of the taxi and started running westbound from the scene. So many things were in my head. "Do I chase the guy, who obviously has a knife, with no back-up? Do I stop and get medical attention for the victim? Do I not get involved because I'm still in the Academy and could easily get fired for making a wrong move?"

I saw others stop to help, so I kept going. I did not have police powers as I had not been sworn-in, which meant I could not chase the guy, and to stay out of trouble, I had to get to work. For weeks, I kept thinking of that situation and questioned if I was afraid to deal with the man with the knife, and if I wasn't afraid, did I still do the right thing?

One thing that experience taught me for sure is to be more precise when faced with adversity and hostile situations. I rarely ever second-guessed myself again. I was always ready to make the best move. And I almost always did.

Murdered in Front of Me

It seemed like being off duty meant that I was going to be a witness to some type of horrific incident. Around 9:00 pm in the summer of 1995, I visited a friend who was having a small social gathering at her Hollywood apartment on Sunset Bl and Hayworth Ave. Since I was a sworn officer, I would always have my firearm and badge in my black leather fanny pack. There were around eight people, socializing and having a good time; suddenly, we heard screams coming from the building next door.

My friend's apartment was facing the street, and a few of us immediately opened the door and walked on the porch to see what the commotion was. Once on the porch, I still heard a woman screaming, "No! Don't do it! Please, come back!" Then I saw a Caucasian man, around twenty-eight to thirty-five years of age, walk across the street carrying what looked like a gun.

Before I could say or do anything besides walk off the porch, the suspect approached a compact vehicle, pointed the gun at the driver, and began firing rounds point-blank into the head of the driver. He shot three times, shattering the glass and causing everybody in the area to become hysterical, screaming, "Oh, my God! He killed him!" I yelled for my friends to call the police! Then it got quiet as he started walking back toward the apartment from where he came from.

By that time, I had made my way in his direction, crouched down behind a car, and watched him from about forty feet away. He was walking with the gun in his waistband; he had a blank stare on his face. Once he stepped on the sidewalk about five feet from me, I stood up with my firearm pointed at him and ordered him to put his hands up. I identified myself as an off-duty police officer while flashing my ID. He complied and put his hands up without saying a word. I approached him, removed the firearm from his waistband, and told him to put his hands on the car that was nearby.

Within a couple of minutes, a sheriff's patrol car arrived with the lights and siren on. The suspect and I never had words, as he was still in a daze, seeming as if he did not care about the consequences of his actions. Once the deputies approached the scene, I immediately informed them that I was an off-duty police officer and that I witnessed the detained suspect commit a murder. I pointed to the car the victim was in, and then I handed the suspect over to the sheriffs.

Once I was done, I went back to the apartment for a moment, where the people at the party were fascinated and jokingly called me a hero. We laughed, and then I left the party to head to my next destination. None of them knew that my emotions were still high related to the treatment that I received from the sheriffs that arrived on the scene. I could not stay around and further discuss how I was feeling. I had just witnessed a murder, apprehended the suspect but still felt extremely uncomfortable around the sheriff's deputies. I had such ill feelings from that encounter alone, so I had to leave.

An Explosion

In the spring of 1996, I was dating a young lady with two daughters who were about eight and ten years old at the time. I was leaving her house with my sixteen-year-old nephew, who I had custody of. It was late, and she and I were having a disagreement, and the kids were tired, so we called it a night. My nephew and I barely said a word all the way from Riverside to West Covina, which was a forty-mile drive.

I suddenly observed a White BMW 320i merge to the right from the fast lane, cutting recklessly across traffic. The same car clipped the back of another vehicle and began to flip, rolling over several times about one hundred and fifty feet in front of me. Once the car came to a stop, it was upside down, started smoking, and caught fire. I stopped and immediately ran toward the accident in the hopes of removing anyone I could from the car. Once at the car, I noticed a bloody arm sticking out of the window, and the vehicle was smashed down to half the normal size. I started pulling on the arm in hopes of extracting the driver when I heard a man crying, "Please, help me!"

As I continued to tug, I realized that it would be a challenge to pull him out of the crushed window because the doors would not open, and the seatbelt was holding him to the seat. Luckily, the fire was burning on top, so I continued pulling, scared as hell the entire time!

Suddenly, there was an explosion. A loud bang! I ran my ass away as fast as I could, thinking I was dead. When I was about forty feet away, I turned around to see the condition of the car. I was trying to determine if it was safe for me to continue rendering aid. Instead, I headed back toward the car once I saw I had not been injured from the explosion, but the flames had spread to the cockpit of the car.

I started pulling again and noticed that the flames were consuming the driver. He was crying louder as I cried, feeling helpless in my efforts to save him. I kept pulling until the cries began to turn into a whisper. The flames engulfed the cabin of the car, and suddenly the whispers became complete silence… the victims were dead. All I could hear was the cracking of embers and sparks stemming from the vehicle being burned. I had never experienced a person dying right in my face.

I went back to my car as the fire department pulled up and began to put out the fire. I sat there for a moment and thanked God for saving my life in the explosion. After praying for the victims, I proceeded to drive home while in complete shock and devastation from witnessing death and not being able to save them.

CHAPTER 8

Here Today, Gone Tomorrow

"There are officers who wake up in the morning with the intent to figure out who they will victimize next."

My neighbors John (RIP) and Lisa Warfield were just like us…a young couple with a newborn baby in a new house, trying to make ends meet. John and I were around the same age at the time, a ripe twenty-eight-years old. However, John acted and had a laugh like an old ass man. I used to tease him all the time. He also had a kind, loving, and helpful spirit, which made him the coolest neighbor ever. What made us grow to be close friends was that he knew people that I knew very well in his old neighborhood near Washington Blvd and 6th Ave. John also went to high school with my wife, and Lisa, a quiet, cute, and very nice person, went to college with me. The fact that we were all neighbors was bizarre. What a small world!

Practically, every day prior to us both going to work, John and I would meet in the driveway and discuss everything from sports to kids to clubbing back in the day. The conversation was engaging, and we always had so much to talk about. One morning, as usual, we started to talk, only John happened to mention that he had an earache. He was not smiling, joking, or in his normal jovial mood, so I knew he was feeling bad. I offered to take him to the doctor, but he responded with, "No, I'll get it checked out later."

I said, "Ok, man. If you need me, I got you."

We both went on with our day, and after that, for the next four days, John did not come out, nor had I seen his wife. I decided to call Lisa and ask how they were doing.

"Oh, I thought you knew. John has been in hospital," she said.

I was blown away because I knew something was wrong, but never did I consider that he would be in the hospital.

"No, I did not. The last time we spoke, he said he had an earache and was going to get it checked out," I responded.

"He did, and they kept him and are running tests." "Sorry to hear that," I said. "Keep me posted."

A few days later, I spoke to Lisa again. "They think he has a tumor on the left side of his brain, and they are still running tests." With a solemn and worried look on her face, she went on to say, "At this point, I'm worried big time because anything on the brain could not be good. However, I prayed he would be okay."

With a new baby, a house, and all the responsibilities associated with dealing with a sick husband, Lisa really had her hands full. The next time I talked to her, which was maybe two days later, she said, "Joe, John is in a coma."

"What the fuck!" I immediately broke down in tears since there was no way I could imagine that I would receive some news like that. "Lisa, I know you told me not to see him, but I think I should," I said.

However, as fast as those words came out of my mouth, I changed my mind, deciding that it may be too much as I was already going through issues on the job, and my heart was not ready to see him.

The following week he was still in a coma, and Lisa said, "Joe, if you want to see him, now would be the time."

I pulled myself together, went to Centinela Hospital, and saw John, but for the life of me, I wished that I never went. The tumor, which was the size of a volleyball, was attached to my friend's head, and it absolutely broke me. To this day, I cannot get the picture of it out of my mind. To see a person who was alive and well one day, and then suddenly God intervenes in a way you would not wish on anybody...it did something to me.

Two weeks after John was laid to rest, Lisa called me to let me know that one day after I went to work, two police cars were at my house, and several officers were taking pictures.

"They went in your backyard, climbed the fence, went in your trash cans, and looked in your windows." She was not sure if they went inside or not. I ascertained that either way, the officers were trespassing since they did not have the right to be on or search my property. At that point, I did not know how to proceed. With all the things I was already dealing with, I was burned out. I knew that no matter how I decided to address it, Lisa would be my only witness, and I was not about to put her through anything after what she had experienced.

I later found out the sergeant who had it out for me regarding my working security without a work permit was the person responsible for the illegal search. My business card said that I had a limo and security service, but what he did not know was that I had a raggedy limo and was aspiring to have a business. With my tenacity and drive, I got the cards before I was ready.

The day that I had the dispute with the sergeant; I wondered why he was so upset about me working without a permit. At that point, I started to think about how my house was shot up after our argument; and now I'm learning about the illegal search of my home. I was starting to believe that the sergeant had a problem with me because he seemed to be the common denominator in every situation.

When we had the dispute about the work permit, I could not figure out for the life of me why he would be so mad over something so small.

"It had to be something else," I thought to myself. "Was he jealous that I had my own business? Was he trying to investigate me to catch me doing something illegal?"

I guess if it walks like a duck and quacks like a duck…it must be a fucking duck! Like I mentioned in the beginning, there are officers that wake up in the morning with an intent to figure out who they will screw or victimize next!

CHAPTER 9

The LA Riots

"It was a crazy feeling I had when having to fight for officers who wrongfully and maliciously beat the hell out of a man who could have easily been me."

I am an entrepreneur to the core, and I am always trying to find a way to make money doing something I enjoy. A few months had passed since the devastating shooting at my home, and I was starting to get back to my old optimistic business-minded self. I did some research and concluded that property ownership brings about generational wealth. I knew that I was not in the position to buy property by myself...at least, I thought it was impossible. I decided to put together a group of around ten men that shared my interest. I believed, with all of us together, we would be able to invest in property. We had our first business meeting at my house on April 29, 1992.

While we were conducting business, we had the television on as we were following the case of the assault on Rodney

King by the LAPD officers. The trial was quite intense. We hoped that the ruling would be in favor of Rodney King since the assault was caught on camera. As the verdicts were read, we were all in disbelief; despite witnesses, video evidence, and the laws that prohibit officers of the law from using excessive force, they were all acquitted. The officers got off!

Every news station began to cover the sites of people in the streets; they were interviewing passersby to get their opinion on the verdict. While reporters were speaking to people on camera, behind the scenes, you could see the developing chaos. Agitation, frustration, anger, and hopelessness were apparent as violence broke out in the streets within minutes. As I watched, I realized that the chaos was on Florence and Normandie, which was about a three-minute drive from my house. The crowd was yelling, screaming, crying, and throwing bottles at cars and trucks passing by. The scene increasingly became dangerous and out of control. I knew that everyone would be upset if things did not go in favor of Rodney King and Black people, who constantly endure injustices. However, it never crossed my mind that the unrest would be to that extent. We were all heartbroken and felt as if our lives did not matter.

I continued to watch as the community grew to be more and more dangerous when all of a sudden, I saw several people stop an eighteen-wheeler and pull Reginald Denny, a White man who just happened to be passing through, out of his truck and proceeded to beat him.

I said, "This is crazy!" I grabbed the take-home rover that the LA Police Department gave me because of the shooting the year prior. "THIS IS ROVER 044! Please, have units respond to Florence and Normandie! They are beating people in the intersection!"

I continued to keep my eyes fixed on the TV, watching the footage being covered by the cameramen. In disbelief, I saw Damian "Football" Williams, who later became one of the LA Four, hit that same White man on his head with a brick.

I yelled in the rover, "Please! Any police units that are in the area of Florence and Normandie…they are Killing people in the Intersection." I continued to beg for the lives of innocent people, "Please, respond C-3!"

Sadly, as I was watching the news, they covered the response from the police, who began retreating to the 77th Division. I was so disappointed to see that none of the units answered the calls of their fellow officers, and even more so, they ignored the citizens of the community that they pledged to serve. Moments later, the city of Los Angeles was on fire, and the looting began. Later that night, the Los Angeles Police Department was mobilized, and I had to go to work.

It is hard to explain the crazy feeling I had when having to fight for officers who wrongfully and maliciously beat the hell out of a man that I felt could have easily been me. From the time we all saw the video, I thought that there was no way in hell they were going to get away with that. I did not care if I was a cop; I wanted the four officers to pay for how they assaulted a man…A Black Man! I saw the video a hundred times, and there was no way anyone could justify the actions of the officers. I am a police officer, but I am a Black man first, and that assault really made me mad. I felt a complete shift and racial divide when it came to the interactions with certain White vs. Black officers due to the tension associated with the heinous act committed by officers and the outcome of the trial. It was obvious that the divisiveness and turmoil were infectious and spreading across the nation.

The tension continued to fester, but sadly, we had a job to do. Working through inflamed political conflict and racial divide takes a toll on you, emotionally and physically. One of the hardest things about the entire situation was having to wear the police uniform when you did not agree with what happened, and Blacks looked at you as if you were a traitor. What they do not know is that Black officers didn't like the shit either, but we had to do our jobs. Hell, there were White officers that hated the unfairness of the trial, and we worked together to do our jobs in hopes of saving the city.

Fires, looting, and protesting…the riots continued for about five days, and I was working twelve hours a day. The city was in chaos! I remember us having three officers in every car and patrolling various zones while watching people loot but not making any arrests. Then there were the business owners in Korea Town, armed with rifles and shotguns, daring people to try and rob them. Unfortunately, there were also shootouts.

Sometimes, there were things we saw that were funny. As we were patrolling near a Fedco Department Store at the cross streets of Rodeo and La Cienega, we saw smoke coming from the building and people running in and out with merchandise. So, my two partners and I decided to go into the store to make sure there were no victims. As soon as we walked into the door, we saw smoke and water everywhere from the sprinkler system. Even though there were police officers in the midst, people continued to steal, running out with all kinds of stuff. We took position behind a wall, and as looters turned the corner, we would jump out, startling them.

"Put that back!"

"AAAAAHHHHHHH!" they would yell.

Stuff went flying everywhere as they would slip, fall, and then get up, running out of the store scared. If there had been surveillance cameras back then, the recordings would have been some of America's funniest videos. The stress was so crazy that it felt good to get a laugh.

After the riots ended, things did not get better right away. There was still tension in the community…eyes rolled every time people saw a cop. There were periodic outbursts of anger and frustration from the division and lack of trust. When it was all said and done, the National Guard was called in to help with the discord. Around sixty-three people lost their lives, there were hundreds of arrests, and there were billions of dollars in property damage.

The city had to be rebuilt, and businesses restored, all because our justice system failed to fairly adjudicate an obvious injustice. A traffic violation turned into a violent violation of a citizen's human rights. Sadly, this time it was caught on tape, and the people of LA still did not get the desired result of justice! It was a slap in the face to Black Americans and every human who believes in fairness and equality.

Due to the civil unrest, a new Chief of Police, Willie Williams, was selected to succeed police chief Daryl Gates on June 30, 1992. Willie Williams, who was not well received by White leaders, was the first Black officer to be sworn in as the police chief of Los Angeles. However, the morale on the job did not get any better. As a Black man who had experienced police harassment prior to becoming an officer, I was frustrated. The situation with Rodney King showed me that America had a serious problem, bigger than anything I could solve—a problem that would not only continue across the nation but also in my career. My status of being a police officer did not mean that I was excluded from racial inequities.

LA Riots

CHAPTER 10

The Notorious Rafael Perez

"As I got closer, I realized it was the entire Vicencio family that was crying, and Jessie, my childhood friend, was lying in a puddle of blood."

Stress is something that impacts the body, and it was evident that I went through a lot. I started having migraine headaches, and my vision was so bad that I thought I was going blind. After seeking medical attention, I found out that the blood vessels burst in my eyes which lead to blurred vision; in fact, I could barely see. I was diagnosed with Central Serous Retinopathy.

1992 was a rough year: My home was shot up; as a result, officers had to provide protection while my family and I slept elsewhere; two people were killed two doors down while the police were parked in my driveway; I was suspended for missing court even though I didn't know about it; a good friend of mine fell ill and died suddenly; then the LA riots occurred. The year was over, and I was still wondering if someone was trying to kill my family and me.

I thought that nothing else would surprise me, but I had no idea what was next in store for me. Dealing with my health and still having to work was extremely difficult, but every day I continued to work and serve the community. Working with the right partner made the job a little easier and a lot more enjoyable. I worked closely with Officer Rafael Perez, and the two of us together were the ideal teammates. We worked mid-days from 10:00 am to 6:00 pm., paired together on the Z-Car, which was a crime suppression car, responding only to serious calls. Together, we received commendations for doing good police work.

Officer Perez was a former Marine; he had developed psychological discipline and combat *skills* through excellent tactical and decision-making *abilities* that did not waiver. The two of us together were like magic, "hooking and booking," as they would say of cops who were making many arrests. We received awards for solving bank robberies, home invasions, and other serious crimes.

Ray Perez was perhaps one of the best cops I had worked with during my entire career, and I had some of my best times fighting crime with him. We began working off-duty jobs together and ultimately became good friends...I was even a groomsman at his wedding.

After about eight months of partnership, Ray was promoted to the West Bureau Crash Unit and then to the Narcotics Buy Team. When he and I worked together, we did good work, and I never witnessed him doing anything wrong or unethical. Since he was working in a new unit, Ray formed new relationships with other officers, including David Mack. Onward, Ray and I only talked periodically.

I first heard of David Mack when I was a sophomore at Crenshaw High School. My first experience with him came from his prowess as an 800m runner for Locke High School. Mack was a rival to a senior at Crenshaw named Jeff West. They were both dynamic athletes and used to battle for the city championship.

I started to get bored with regular patrol and was looking for an opportunity that would expose me to other areas so I could eventually move up the ranks. I spoke to Ray about it, and he suggested that I join the Buy Team and that he would put in a good word for me. I submitted a transfer and had pretty much been accepted. I had to wait for the deployment period to end the transition over, but what I did not know was that that day would never happen. What transpired next was something I never imagined.

October 26, 1993, was a day that I would never forget since it changed the trajectory of my career. While on routine patrol in Wilshire Division, a call came over the radio. "Shots Fired with a Man Down" near Harvard Blvd and Cambridge. I just happened to be leaving the station and recognized the call was right around the corner from where I grew up. I took the call and responded, "Code-3," with lights and siren on.

When I arrived, I saw a few people in the area, and then I noticed the body lying in the street. My partner and I stopped about twenty feet away from the victim and drew our weapons since we did not know if the suspects were still around. As I got closer, I realized it was the entire Vicencio family crying, and Jessie, my childhood friend, was lying in a puddle of blood.

When the family saw that I was one of the officers, Jessie's mother yelled in a hysterical rant over and over, "Jrrrrrrrrrr! They killed my baby!"

I momentarily gasped for breath as I looked down; Jessie was fighting to breathe with multiple gunshots. The scene was unbelievable and seemed like a nightmare. Jessie's wife was going crazy, trying to get to him from the front porch of the house, and all I could think about was that I needed to stop her from seeing him. I had no idea what happened or who shot Jessie, but I just knew what I had to do.

As I moved toward the family, I told them, "Please, go into the house. You don't need to see this."

Before I knew it, a Black detective in plainclothes approached Jessie's wife as she collapsed in anguish. I thought that he was going to console her; instead, he started pulling her by her feet and up the stairs. At that point, a large group of neighbors was crowding around. It would have been a terrible look for me to seem like I was okay with the detective dragging a woman that was obviously grieving, so I told him, "Hey, let me handle them. I am the only person they will listen to." He stopped, let go of her feet, and allowed me to get Jessie's wife and family into the house.

Everyone was crying and screaming, and before I knew it, the wife went around me and went back on the porch trying to get to Jessie. Suddenly, the detective grabbed her again and dragged her while cursing and yelling for her to move.

I told him again, "Look! I told you I got the fucking family. I can't explain right now but let me handle it."

He was obviously pissed at me, but I am sure he did not realize the consequences I was facing if I didn't intervene. My father still lived right around the corner, and many of the people knew us both. I wanted to defuse the situation without retaliation to my family.

Jessie and I met when we were nine or ten years old. We grew up around the corner from each other, and I knew his entire family...his father Jessie Sr., his mother Gloria, his brother Michael, and his little sister Jenina. I used to pass their house every day walking to Normandie Park in our neighborhood, and the family would always be so nice and loving to me. They would feed me like I was their own son, and I even spent the night at their house a few times.

Jessie was crazy as fuck...even as a kid. One day, when I was twelve years old, I rode to the market with the family. We were near a gang-infested area at Olympic and Redondo, waiting in front of the store while Jessie's parents were inside picking up items they needed. While we were waiting in the car, three young Latino boys approached us and started an argument with Jessie. They were yelling back and forth, "Fuck you! We will kick your ass!"

Although I witnessed everything and had no clue what they were mad about, I was going down with my homie, so I joined the argument. When things started to get heated, Jessie's mom and dad came out and calmed things down. As they were walking away, they kept saying, "We coming back aye. With sticks and stones aye."

We pulled off, and crazy ass Jessie was laughing and said, "Joe Jr., I didn't know you get mad." I told him that he has never seen me mad because he never messed with me.

As time went on, we were still friends, but Jessie started gang banging for the C-14 Clanton Mexican Street Gang. They rivaled against the eighteenth street gang, Harpies, Mid-City, and Mara Salvatrucha. Later, he became a major member of the El Salvadorian gang known to kill, sell drugs, and raise hell in the neighborhood…even to this very day.

By the time we were fourteen, we rarely saw each other because my parents put me in sports, so I was always at practice. Sports tore me away from my other friends that were doing little odd crimes as well. I will be the first to say that sports saved me from getting caught up in a life of crime.

Jessie later became one of the leaders, known killer, and dope dealer in the C-14 Gang, and I turned out to be an average but continuously improving athlete and student who stayed out of trouble. So, imagine the day of the "Shots Fired" radio call in my old hood.

Arriving and seeing Jessie riddled with bullets, his family crying their eyes out, and his mother saying, "They killed my baby! They killed my baby! Oh, God!" This situation, even up until today, was the most tragic experience I have ever had.

After the immediate roar of this toxic situation, I found out that Jessie was killed by undercover narcotics officers. Ray Perez and David Mack were working in the undercover Buy Unit that I was already approved to transfer to the following month. I later talked to Ray about what happened, and he said they were sent to buy drugs as they got word that sells were being made in the area. He and Mack pulled up and asked Jessie where they could get some dope.

He said, "Jessie appeared to be high on something, took out a gun, and began waving it saying, 'You guys ain't Bloods, are you?' Jessie was standing behind Mack on the driver's side and kept repeating, 'You mutha fuckers ain't Bloods, are you?' I began talking to Jessie from the passenger side of the car to divert his attention, and while Jessie was looking at me, Mack pulled his 9mm from his jacket, turned toward Jessie, and began firing rounds in his chest." Jessie collapsed in the street, and that is when my partner and I pulled up. At that point, Mack and Perez were both removed from the scene.

When a friend kills a friend, it is a strange and difficult pill to swallow. I knew that I could not take sides. All I could do was get the facts and pray that God protects all involved. I knew the killers of Jessie Vicencio, but I don't know if he was armed or not. I never saw a gun or any proof he had one.

Imagine that day when I heard the "Shots Fired" radio call in my old neighborhood. I anticipated that there was a possibility that the person shot would be someone I knew, but it never crossed my mind that it would be someone that I was close to. Arriving on the scene and seeing Jessie full of bullet holes and his family crying their eyes out is something I will never forget. The grieving screams were heart wrenching as they poured their pain on my shoulders.

"Jrrrrrrrrrrrr," his mom screamed, "They killed my baby! They killed my baby! Oh, God!"

No one other than people in my family or extremely close to me could call me Jr. The Vicencios were obviously like family to me, and to this day, the murder of Jessie was the most tragic experience I have ever had. Although our journey in life took us in opposite directions, we were tied with unconditional love. Jessie was a gang banger and a menace to society and to the police, but he was crazy ass Jessie to me. A crazy person I loved was killed by two police officers I knew. It was never about choosing sides.

The next day, the detective that oversaw the Buy Team called me in his office. I will never forget him saying, "Due to that situation related to the shooting, you created some bad blood in the Buy Unit. I know you're supposed to come here next month, but you will need to apologize to the unit, and even then, I still can't promise that you will be accepted."

I responded, but not like he probably thought I would. "Sir, I did not do anything negative. I tried to explain that the circumstances were not normal to your D-2, but he did what he did anyway. I'm okay…I don't have to join the unit. Thank you for considering me." The stress was continuing to build, and I thought I was dying a slow death.

Later that day, a sergeant who knew my character said that the same D-2 (Detective 2) was telling anyone who would listen that I took the gang banger's side at an officer-involved shooting. He never tried to understand the truth of where I stood. I knew both sides and had no motive to choose one over the other. I was just trying to defuse an ugly situation without putting my family in jeopardy.

I never recovered from what I considered to be a nightmare. After that, the sergeants seemed to have it out for me. The stares I started getting were so intense that I felt that it was truly time to consider moving away from police work. I did not trust my safety with that type of negativity floating around. This horrific situation was never about choosing sides. That is when I realized…they never trained me for this in the academy.

CHAPTER 11

Off Duty Shenanigans

""He said, 'Joe, I'm in some trouble! I know you heard about that Snoop Shooting; I'm the one who shot that guy! I promise it was self-defense!"

The ups and downs of being a police officer took me through hell and back. The fear and paranoia for my wife's wellbeing had set in since my house was shot up, so I decided there was no way my family could continue to live in our home. A coworker, Steven Smith, happened to be managing off-duty law enforcement officers in a large apartment complex in Torrance. His job was to find officers that would agree to provide security for a few days a month in exchange for a discount on the rent. This opportunity was right up my alley at the time. I had to get my wife and son out of the city anyway, and Torrance was a good exodus for us, so we moved and rented out our home.

The things that happened once in Torrance were wild, so I apologize now to my officer friends included in this story. Nothing incriminating…just fun mixed with tragedies, scandals, and violence.

Not long after moving to Torrance, I began to take on as much off-duty work as I could find so I could buy another house for my family. One of the jobs was security for the Lakewood Red Onion. The spot was hot! It was frequented by players from Long Beach, Compton, Lakewood, Bellflower, and surrounding areas. It was an All-Black crowd, and some people were dressed down like tough, hardcore gangsters, and others were cool and professional- looking men. DJ Black was the DJ who was known to keep the crowd happy.

Then we had the likes of Snoop Dogg, Warren G, Nate-Dogg, and other rappers who would stop in. There was a wide variety of sexy, down, open- minded women that came from Hawthorne, Los Angeles, and Orange County, in addition to the sexy ladies from the hood. Police officers never had problems pulling the ladies, but sad to say that most of the crew was in situationships or marriages, and my ass was one of them.

Our crew consisted of police officers that included me, Rafael Perez, Steve Smith, and Compton officers Sanford and Hamilton. Then we had security guards that worked for the Red Onion. The security guard that stood out in my mind was Malik, whose real name was McKinley Lee. Malik was a very well put together brother who was Muslim, about five foot, eleven inches, and two hundred and twenty pounds of muscle. I immediately took him under my wing because he was professional, well-spoken, and knew martial arts. Yes, that meant he could whip ass! Heck, our whole crew was no joke!

We stuck to our mission, which was to keep the knuckleheads from acting up, kick ass only when needed, and satisfy the ladies on a routine basis. But every now and then, it simply had to go down.

One weekend we had a large crowd, and we enforced a strict dress code consisting of no jeans and t-shirts. A fella, who was in line with four to five other guys, wore jeans, so he was advised that we had a no jean policy. He insisted on being let in, so I personally handled him as he became too big of a fish for the regular security to handle.

I said nicely, "Sir! You can't come in. Can you please step to the side?"

He started getting louder, saying, "Man, these are Girbaud Jeans. They cost more than anything you have on!"

I said, "My man, they are some nice jeans, but you can't get in with them."

Before I knew it, the crew was right there with me, and then the guy made the mistake of getting too close to me. I extended my arm and said, "Don't come past my zone again."

This stupid fool took a step toward me, and I immediately felt threatened, so I hit him in the face, and the fight was on.

We ended up fighting with him and his friends. Ray punched one of them, Sandford slapped one with his big ass hands, and Steve got some punches in as well. What's funny is all I remember was Malik flipping one of the guys multiple times all over the parking lot, and the guy kept screaming, "STOP! STOP!"

I was like, "Damn! That Boy can go!"

Before we knew it, the guys got out of there, and no arrests were made. Just ass kicked and respect gained.

Most nights after the club, we would meet females at Norms for breakfast about a half mile away. Our entire crew had a thing for the ladies, and we were honestly like magnets. I hate to give details on another man's transgressions, so I will just say that we had it going on. However, one night, which was only a few out of many, was a night gone bad. After Norms, I followed a female friend home to Orange County, knowing that I should have taken my tired ass home, but I went anyway.

Her place seemed to be underground since the windows were up above, and there was only one way out. After spending time, I heard a male voice come from one of the upper windows calling the female's name, asking to let in. I woke her up, and we saw the guy trying to peek in the windows. I immediately armed myself with my 9mm handgun and assessed who the guy was.

She said, "It's my ex-boyfriend."

I told her not to say anything. He moved around to other windows but could not see inside. I thought he would break a window and come in, so I was already devising a plan. The last thing I wanted was for anything to happen, knowing my sorry ass should have been home with my wife. He called her name a couple more times, and then thankfully, he left. As soon as I felt the coast was clear, I got out of there and never went back.

I have so many more stories about the Lakewood Red Onion, but I will end with this one. One night, I was asleep at home with my wife, and I got a late- night call. Heck, I was afraid to answer it. It turned out to be Malik from the club. I was grooming Malik to become a police officer, so I made myself available to him no matter what was going on.

He said, "Joe! Man, I'm in some trouble. I know you heard of the shooting Snoop was involved in last night."

I said, "Yes, I heard."

He said, "Joe, I'm the one who shot the guy!" He continued to tell me the story, and I could tell that he was scared and did not know what to do. "Joe, I promise it was self-defense. That guy was coming up to the van with all of us in it, pointing a gun. I told him to stop, but he kept getting closer, so I shot him." He explained that he responded that way because he knew the guy was a gang banger. "I'm scared and don't know what to do."

I asked, "So, you've been running?"

"Yes!" He sounded so lost and scared at the same time.

I said, "Malik, you need to contact a lawyer, tell him exactly what happened, and have him turn you in immediately. The longer you run, the more they will assume you are guilty."

Malik turned himself in the next morning, and they kept him in jail until the trial was over. Initially, it was said that the gang member, Phillip Woldemarian, did not have a gun. Then later, it was revealed the gun had been hidden. Both Snoop and McKinley Lee, aka Malik, were acquitted of the murder. I never saw Malik again, but in my gut, I knew he was telling the truth because of everything he showed me prior to the situation taking place.

Wise, Wiggins & Jones – Officers at the Wilshire Plantation

CHAPTER 12

A Celebrity Crime Scene

"I began to really think OJ killed his ex-wife and her friend. However, I was willing to let the facts prevail."

With the police force leaders being part of ostracizing and mistreating me, my stress level increased tremendously, and I did not know what to expect from the people around me. I already saw misuse and abuse of the badge on so many occasions. The LA Riot brought so much additional discord to the police department and contributed to how I was starting to feel about the organization.

The citizens of Los Angeles were not pleased with the Chief of Police, Daryl Gates. Just like the chief that preceded him, Gates did not seem to believe that community involvement with civil rights activists was necessary. He was blamed for the atrocities imposed on citizens throughout his tenure as a leader and later he decided to retire after the devastating unrest in the city. So, on June 30, 1993, Willie

Williams was appointed as Chief of Police. He may have thought that the aftermath of the LA Riots would be the worst situation he would encounter, but little did he know, another tragedy would shake up the city and inflame the already present racial divide.

The tension at the Wilshire division had become so intense that I considered quitting the job, but deep down, I wanted to stay, so I transferred to the WLA Division in hopes of salvaging my career by working a 3 to 12 condensed work schedule. As soon as I arrived at WLA, it seemed like the shit hit the fan.

On June 12, 1994, Nicole Brown Simpson and Ron Goldman were tragically murdered. It was announced that night while I was out partying, and I remember having a candid conversation with a couple of people at the party about the situation. I was not having the discussion as an officer but as a person who understood the issues with having children in a dysfunctional relationship. My initial thought was, "Awe shit! Where is OJ?"

I, unfortunately, thought of him as a suspect as soon as I heard, and I didn't give a shit what color he was. I ended up leaving the party early because somehow, I knew it was going to be a busy day. Lo and behold, I was on the scene on Bundy Avenue five hours later.

The bodies had just been removed, leaving an extremely bloody mess. Blood ran from past the inside of the gate and continued down the pavement to the outside of the fence. Numerous detectives and officers were still at the location when my partner and I arrived, and OJ had not been announced as a suspect at the time. I, like everyone else, was lost as to exactly what transpired and who really murdered them. As details were discovered, I began to really think OJ killed his wife and her wife's friend. However, I was prepared to let the facts prevail.

Then on June 17th, he and Al Cowlings were being pursued by the police in the infamous Bronco car chase. I assumed OJ was guilty at that point. If not, why would he run and contemplate suicide? However, after all the evidence was laid out by Johnny Cochran, revealing that blood was transferred to OJ's house, curiosity was built across the world. This changed the narrative and became all about race. White people wanted OJ to be found guilty, and Blacks wanted him to be innocent. Based on the historical fate of Black men in court and the passion the White officers demonstrated in finding him guilty, the work environment was crazy. The trial was another incident that displayed the racial divide in the country.

Walkway to Bundy Dr. minutes after bodies were removed (Me)

CHAPTER 13

A Nightmare in Hollywood

"I thought I wanted to die that day; I would never recover from this. I felt I could never trust the police or courts again."

I transferred to the WLA Division seeking a new start after encountering so many issues at the Wilshire Division. However, I was still promoting events whenever I was off duty. On December 27th, 1995, around 10:30 pm, I went to drop off invitations to a close family friend and fellow police officer, Daryn Dupree. He was a detective in training that I recruited to join the LA Police Department. He was working as the doorman off-duty for a popular nightclub, The Roxbury on Sunset Blvd.

When I arrived at the club, it was extremely crowded. I drove up and down Sunset Blvd. looking for a parking space. I could not find one, so I circled around just near the front of the club and asked the attendant how much it was to park. I believe he said $25. It was a huge mistake on my part not to pay for parking. Instead, I decided to park next to a hot dog vendor. Since I was not blocking the driveway, I thought to myself, "I'll only be a minute. I'll just park here and run in."

Once at the front door, I saw Officer Dupree, so we spoke for a few minutes while I observed the scene. He started to tell me a story about a fight that occurred at the club the previous week involving Suge Knight and a guy that was a well-known local dope dealer. Dupree told me the dope dealer, who was said to be a black belt in karate, and Suge fought, and the dealer got the best of him, fighting Suge with a derby hat on the entire time. It was a fascinating story due to Suge's tough-guy reputation with Death Row Records, but it extended my short stay to fifteen minutes. After I heard the story, I gave Dupree the invitations and left.

As I was leaving the club, I approached the hot dog vendor that was directly next to my car to buy a hot dog before I pulled off. As soon as I began to order from her, I saw a Sheriff's black and white vehicle pull behind my car, and a large White male officer with a thick mustache exited and approached on the driver's side. Knowing that I was illegally parked, I stepped off the curb to get in my car and leave. As I stepped off the curb, the deputy said in an extremely hostile manner, "Get back on the fucking curb! Is this your car?"

I said, "Yes, I'm about to leave right now."

"No, you're not! Your fucking car is getting towed! You've been parked here for forty-five minutes!"

"No, I haven't. I've only been here for fifteen minutes."

In apparent frustration that I corrected him, he replied, "I don't care, your car is getting towed."

At that point, with him being so hostile, I removed my police badge from my black leather fanny pack in hopes of presenting it to him and defuse the situation. I said, "Sir, I'm not trying to be a problem. Look…I'm an officer too! I do the same thing you do."

As I was presenting my ID to him, he looked up and abruptly tried to snatch the ID out of my hand. I guess he didn't know that it was wrapped around my hand by a small silver chain. I said, "What are you doing?"

Simultaneously, he was removing his gun from his holster, pointed it directly at my face from about two feet away, and said, "Get your fucking hands up before I blow your head off!" He went on to yell, "If you're a cop, that means you have a gun in that bag!"

I immediately dropped my fanny pack and the ID, and I began to plead with the officer not to shoot me. I said, "Sir, I'm a police officer! I told you who I was, so why are you doing this?"

With the look of hate in his eyes, he said, "I don't give a fuck!"

I just stood there with my hands up, thinking this crazy ass sheriff might kill me. I was in total fear for my life.

The officer proceeded to request backup for "a man with a gun." I was so scared that I started looking around, asking people that I had never seen in my life to please stay and witness what was happening. I said, "Please, don't leave. I'm afraid for my life!"

A few people stayed, but others kept walking. At the same time, an LA Police Department car was passing, so the Deputy with the gun in my face flagged them down. The officers did a U-turn and got out of their black and white vehicle. Soon after, four or five Sheriff vehicles, with lights and sirens blaring, pulled up, making a huge scene. I was standing with my hands against the car as I was ordered, and suddenly there was one more LA Police Department unit with two more White officers from my department.

The deputy asked the four White police officers, "Is this an LA Police ID legitimate?"

As he held up my identification for feedback from the officers, they responded, "Yes."

He said, "Yeah, Right," as though he did not believe them. "Is this a weapon your department is authorized to carry?" He showed them my off-duty Smith and Wesson 9mm.

"Yes," they responded. The officer appeared to be even more bothered. He acted as if there was no way a Black man could be an officer.

I was quiet, afraid, and embarrassed as a large crowd formed around the scene. Even though they had plenty of evidence that I was an officer, they handcuffed me and placed me in the back of a sheriff's car. As they were cuffing me, the deputies were taunting me. The one who put the handcuffs on put them on wrong and turned them to ensure they gouged into my wrist to cause pain.

I said to him, "This is fucked up! You guys are going to have to answer for this."

As I sat in the back of the police car, it took everything for me not to tear up out of anger. I thought I was about to die at the hands of a fellow officer for parking illegally. The complete humiliation I felt as an officer and as a Black man...I could not believe I was being treated like a criminal. After ten minutes, the LA police officers came to the car to talk to me. I immediately asked them to request a sergeant from the West LA Division to investigate and talk to witnesses because I knew the sheriffs would lie about what happened.

The police officers told me that the deputy who arrested me was an asshole, and he did not believe them when they said my ID was real and my gun was authorized. They told me not to worry; they were requesting a sergeant. The sergeant arrived around thirty minutes later and investigated the scene by questioning the witnesses. There were no complaints made against me by the deputies and the LA police officers, nor was it said that I did anything wrong besides parking in a red zone, for which I took full responsibility.

Stories Change

I could not live with the way I was treated, so while I was at work the following Monday, I contacted the Sheriff's Station and spoke to the Watch Commander to report the misconduct against the officers who were involved in mistreating me. After reporting the situation, I waited patiently while continuing to salvage my career at my new station. Two to three months went by without any word from the Sheriff's Department, leaving me to feel abandoned by the organization that I initially was honored to be a part of. At the time, a simple apology from the deputies would have at least cured my heart. I never received a response, and no one took responsibility.

About five months after my civil rights were violated and the sheriffs obviously swept my complaint under the rug, I filed a lawsuit against all deputies involved. The pain and disappointment became too much to bear. To be ignored caused me a great deal of apprehension about continuing within law enforcement. After the Sheriff's Department received the lawsuit, they filed a retaliatory personnel complaint against me, alleging that my conduct was unbecoming of an officer while on the scene on December 27th. This complaint was made eight months after the incident occurred and was made as direct revenge for the lawsuit that was filed against them.

As a total contradiction to what being decent is about, the LA Police Department reopened the investigation, even though an investigation was conducted by a sergeant the night they absolved me from any wrongdoing. This complaint completely stripped me of any trust I had left for them. The four sheriffs involved all conspired and had similar stories claiming I acted out the night of the incident. However, none of these accusations made their way into the sergeant's investigation the night it occurred.

On the contrary, the four White police officers who worked at an entirely different station, of whom I had never met, all stated that I cooperated with the sheriffs the entire time and that I was not rude or disruptive. Two of the officers stated both in the first and second investigation that the deputy was very provoking and rude to them by his gestures and comments like 'Yeah right!' when he asked them if the ID and gun were official items authorized by the LA Police Department.

As far as the witnesses that stood by and watched, there were three people who were interviewed that I had never met before. One was a Black male, one Hispanic older woman, and a White male parking attendant; they all gave statements that supported my version of the story. None of their accounts matched the sheriff's version of what occurred.

The final independent witness was a Black female who went to my high school. Initially, she did not even approach and make a statement. I just happened to notice her in the crowd. I had not seen her in about fourteen years and had to do some research to locate her to get her testimony. Even from the beginning, her statements did not offer much support. She just made the comment that she did not know who the Black man was, but he appeared to be getting harassed by the cops. She did not claim to know more and never stepped up to provide a story. She simply bowed out, citing having personal problems.

The ethics of law enforcement was nonexistent as they found it beneficial for the four sheriffs named in the lawsuit to show a unified front and lie about what transpired. On the contrary, there were the four police officers, whose testimony supported my story, the independent witnesses whose story backed my version of what happened, and the Sergeant made it clear that no one had complained against me that night. All overwhelming evidence to support my case and the Captain still classified my complaint as "Unfounded," meaning they could not prove the case one way or the other.

The entire situation had me completely upset. For the sheriffs to be so malicious in their actions, and not having the support of my department, was a terrible feeling. All I had was the hope of the lawsuit vindicating me for how I was treated. The mishandling of the situation caused me to need psychological counseling to continue as an officer and prevent depression.

The Trial

After being at WLA for about a year, I went back to the Wilshire Division, and in 1996 the trial began. It was a long two-month process. New depositions were taken, testimonies were given, and somehow, stories changed. The sheriff's account of what transpired contained the consistent lies they told from the very beginning. My story and the independent witnesses' account remained the same as well. However, for a reason to this very day I could not understand, the police officer's testimonies changed. The two officers who previously testified to support that I had done no wrong were suddenly speaking as though they were not as sure as they had been in previous statements. Both officers, a male and a female, were so persuasive that I believed they had done enough for the jury to be confused or to simply think that I had acted inappropriately that night.

To put it point blank, the LA police officers lied on behalf of the sheriff. At the time, my primary attorney, Huge Manes, started to be absent for a few of my court dates. So, his assistant attorney handled several days of valuable trial time. This lady was an older person who was not professional in her appearance in any way. She wore old clothes, did not comb her hair in styles consistent with court acumen, and she appeared to be intimidated by the process. All of a sudden, this is who I was stuck with for the most important trial of my life.

I personally had to devise the plan to discredit the police officer's testimony by reminding her that, although discovery had been completed and we had to base testimony on the depositions, we had to show the judge the police officer's previous testimony documented during the official personnel investigation, and how it was different from what they said in court. After reading the investigation, she decided to follow my direction.

The following day in court, the assistant attorney presented the new evidence to the judge. After reading the previous testimony by the police officers, the Judge had to make a special ruling before the jury. The judge stated, "For the inference of justice," the discovery process had to be bypassed, and the personnel complaint had to be read as evidence by the jury so the truth would be known. The police officers had been caught changing their testimony by the judge and jury.

As God would have it, I won my case as the jury determined 12-0 that I was illegally detained and deadlocked 6-6 as it pertained to malice. Nonetheless, although the jury sided in my favor, the court asked them to name who was responsible for the illegal detention. The options were the deputy who initiated the situation and threatened to kill me with his gun, the deputy who cuffed me inappropriately, causing injury and pain to my wrists before putting me in the car, and the sergeant who arrived after I had a gun pointed at me and after the illegal detention and handcuffing occurred.

Somehow, after the verdict had already been rendered and the case won in my favor, the Sheriff's counsel took advantage of an opportunity to not make the officers accountable for their actions. This was a pivotal and climactic moment of the trial, and the attorney I hired was still not available. Subsequently, for some strange reason, the jury picked the sergeant as the person responsible for what happened to me. Therefore, justice was not served on my behalf. Legally, a sergeant cannot be held liable for decisions made in the process of police activity while supervising officers. Since the Sheriff's counsel added the sergeant's name, knowing he could not be liable, my case was declared a mistrial.

A year of pain and suffering, two months of court on a daily basis while listening to the lies and slander of my name, and several months of being in a financial bind…I received nothing. My rights, proven by a jury to have been violated, and suddenly, a Black man, a Black officer, a broken man, a human being who was seeking due process or even a simple apology, was kicked out of court so that the next trial could begin. It was the worst feeling ever. I thought I wanted to die that day. I would never recover from this. I felt I could never trust the police or courts again.

CHAPTER 14

Officer Down

"A couple of days before Kevin was killed, we had a conversation, and he told me he was being followed by the police."

Kevin Gaines and I met through a long-time mutual friend of mine, retired officer Derwin Henderson. Subsequently, we ended up working together as fellow officers at the West LA Station. We also went to lunch and hung out on multiple occasions. He used to attend several of my events, so I knew his wife, daughters, and even after his divorce, I became acquainted with his girlfriend, who was also Suge Knight's ex-wife. I am not sure how he ended up with Suge's ex-wife, but it happened.

On March 18, 1997, Officer Kevin Gaines was killed in Studio City, California. I knew that he was in trouble, but I never thought that it would amount to death. A couple of days before Kevin was killed, we had a conversation, and he told me that he was being followed by the police. He did not make it known to the officers that he knew he was being followed, and he did not mention why they were after him. The only thing he said was that he and his girlfriend sued the Los Angeles Police Department for illegally searching her Hollywood Hills residence.

When I heard the news that Kevin was killed, I knew that he was targeted and murdered but wondered why it was necessary to kill him. At that point, I was officially afraid of law enforcement. To know that my friend was being hunted and was now dead was a scary fucking thing. To see his little girls and wife at the funeral made it even more painful.

The documented reason for the death of Kevin Gaines was road rage. Sadly, like it's done, they slandered his name to make him appear like a dirty cop. If it was not for a motormouth killer speaking on what happened while being secretly taped, the truth might not have ever come out. That killer was an undercover sergeant who was later caught bragging on tape about killing Kevin Gaines.

He said, "The only thing I regret was that there were no more people in the car to kill." The investigation into the murder of Kevin Gaines resulted in the uncovering of police corruption.

Over seventy officers were implicated in police misconduct to include beatings, shootings, bank robberies, planting of evidence on innocent people, and dealing of illegal drugs. Not only were they accused of immoral acts, but they also committed perjury and covered up evidence that would lead to convictions. The Rampart Scandal, as it was known, led to a few of the officers being convicted, some were forced to resign, and a handful of them were terminated. At the end of it all, the convictions were overturned, but there were $125 million in settlements from the lawsuits filed against the city. To be clear, Kevin was not part of the scandal.

Kevin was confident, loved his daughters dearly, and was a family man. He was also someone that would stand up for himself. We never got over the Rodney King beating that was caught on tape, and now this…a Black officer was killed by a White officer, fueling racial tensions even more.

CHAPTER 15

PTSD by Blue

"I know for a fact, Police Brutality, Racism, and Injustice Encounters leave a lasting effect on the victims."

This will be the hardest part of my law enforcement life to talk about because it involves me trying to figure out why I was no longer in total control of my thoughts, emotions, and attitude—the point where I realized I was broken, damaged, and outside of myself. I will just say it. Based on mental evaluations from several psyche doctors, it was concluded that the job gave me PTSD (Post Traumatic Syndrome Disorder). It was some shit I fought real hard not to accept. I had always prided myself on being strong. My family raised me to be strong.

In my early life, it was proven that my mental game was tight. I always stood tall in adversity. I was always a leader. I had poise and was always a clutch performer in all I did. At times, I had normal fears but faced them head- on. Then like a movie, I never had a chance to the premier; traumatic situation after traumatic situation took a toll that caused me to be different. I was depressed, I was having headaches, I lost vision in my eyes due to blood vessels bursting because of stress. Everything was cloudy and out of focus. I became fearful, anxious, hateful, sad, and extremely untrusting.

I was still wearing a blue uniform and living a lie, trying to force myself to believe in things about being a police officer that I could no longer believe. The very sight of a White male figure in a uniform or a black and white police car made me increasingly uncomfortable, anxious, and fearful. I was suddenly in a world that I received extreme joy from, to a world I hated to face daily. I was given pills I was supposed to take to help me cope. I did the opposite and did not take them. If I had taken them, in my mind, it would have been validation that I was officially crazy. If I needed them or not, it was not happening. Not that I didn't need some temporary help. However, I was too prideful and old-school. I was not taking any goddamn pills! The plan was to keep living until these fears and anxieties would go away. Thirty years later, my anger, depression, emotions, fears, physical issues, and trust factors are still present. Less extreme, but are still present.

I was trying to pinpoint when the trauma occurred. So many scenarios took place where I felt helpless and majorly afraid. How would I have known it occurred? Because let's face it, I was a big, bad cop! I was invincible, and Lord knows I was not supposed to be afraid of anything, especially another officer. Hell, we were on the same team, right? I took an oath and had a badge and gun just like they did. If anything happened, they would have my back and vice versa?

Feeling the fear of dying, being harmed, conspired against, and simply unsupported at some point during my eight years as an officer did a number on me. I can't say exactly when. All I can say is it happened. I was a changed man. The slightest wrong move toward me would cause me to lash out.

My disposition caused me to want to work alone. This was the only remedy I knew to prolong my career at the time. I refused to quit. I worked a U-Car (report writing car) for the last months of my career. I was doing my job and staying from most officers for the most part because, at that time, I had no idea who I could trust. While on duty, I received a call that my son was not feeling well. So, as I normally do, between calls or while call code-7 (Lunch), I filled out uncompleted reports.

This particular day, I took C-7 and went to make sure my son was doing well as we lived on the border of the division. While doing reports and spending time with my sick son, my radio battery died. I had not realized my battery was dead until I completed the reports some forty-five minutes to an hour later.

When I got in my police vehicle, I received a code-1 from Dispatch, meaning to respond to the operator immediately! I responded and was asked what my location was. I stated I was on my way to the station as it was close to the end of watch for me anyway, and I wanted to get back to caring for my son. A Sergeant then requested my location while I was driving.

Once again, I stated, "on my way to the station." The same Sergeant then said in an aggressive tone, "Stop where you are!"

By this time, I was two minutes away from the station in the middle of traffic. If I stopped where I was, I would cause an accident, and I simply did not think he realized I was about to arrive, so I continued heading to the station. Once I was at the station, I come in and immediately see what the emergency was. I was met by several White supervisors, two sergeants, and a lieutenant huddled up in the watch commander's office as though they were planning a lynching.

In an aggressive tone, one of them asked me, "Why didn't you respond?"

I told them that my battery died on my radio, and I did not hear them call until I got in the car. A different sergeant then began to question me about a few old reports that had not been finalized. As I've said, my attitude was not the best at all when it came to dealing with officers, especially supervisors, so I felt overwhelmed by them surrounding me and asking me questions in an accusatory manner about some old ass reports that I had nothing to do with. Those reports were an oversight by officers from the previous shift. They had this look of 'We got your ass, and now, it's time to pay!'

I was so upset since I knew I had done nothing wrong, and they were fucking with me. At that point, I told them all, "I don't know what all this assuming I did something wrong is all about, but those are some old reports that have been in the box for two days because the registered owner could not be located. I haven't done nothing but handle the calls I was given. If you figure out that I have done something wrong, you know what to do! I'm out of here!" and I stormed out, went to clean out the police car, and got dressed. Then I got in my personal car and never put that uniform on again. I concluded that there was a conspiracy, and the lies that were being told had all the supervisors trying to get me, all working together to get rid of the Brother.

Knowing that I was overwhelmed and unfit to continue dealing with the continued onslaught of conspiracies and racial tension, I sought a psyche doctor that represented police officers the next day. The hell that I had been through was well documented due to so many terrible things happening in such a short time. The PTSD had taken full flight on my life. I was a sensitive, angry and depressed individual. The doctor I was seeing recommended I have a 5150 Hold placed on me and stay at the LA County Psychiatric Ward simply for evaluation.

I initially said no because I did not have any idea of the seriousness of what I was feeling, nor the effects it could have; I decided to go out of fear. I had already left my wife due to my inability to cope with a relationship, so I was clear to go to the ward on my own merits.

What a weird fucking feeling. One minute I'm placing 5150 Holds on suspects and victims, then all of a sudden, I've changed to being an officer who questioned if it was safe not placing a hold on myself. It was the lowest point of my life. I honestly did not know how life would be like moving forward. I was a scared victim unknowingly, now imagining what regular Black men feel when overwhelmed and victimized by the police.

I stayed at the ward for two of the three days I was supposed to. I participated in some of the counseling and group sessions as well as the interventions. I soon realized that by pride and ego alone, I was not staying another moment in that place. I was going to figure it out somehow, but not at a psyche ward, so I checked out early.

Nonetheless, I know for a fact, based on Black officer retention and Black male suicides and mental health issues, that police brutality, racism, and injustice encounters leave a lasting effect on the victims. I'm willing to bet thousands of Black people are thinking they are living normal lives who have been the victim of an overwhelming officer, currently have a psychological defect because of one or many negative encounters with law enforcement or the courts. It is time to start helping these people as opposed to continuing to suppress and victimize them. It is sad that so many Black officers and Black Americans have to be afraid of police who are sworn to protect them.

CHAPTER 16

White Privilege

"Both Deputies approached with an entirely different attitude. They had their guns pointed at me saying, 'Get your hands up, Get your hands up!'"

As of July 1997, I was no longer a police officer. I had come to the conclusion that it takes a different type of person to be a devoted police officer. One who will leave his pride, ethics, and principles of morality at the door because many times, you are expected to turn a blind eye. I actually thought they wanted me because I was honest. Turns out they didn't.

One would think in a normal situation, when you leave one profession to enter another, that it is a simple process of doing what is necessary to make the transition happen. Unfortunately, with the police, I left with so much baggage that it became difficult. I was past 100 pounds overweight; I had injuries to my foot, toe, knee, neck, and back. I had migraines, episodes of blindness, and PTSD that I previously spoke of. The police officer thing was extremely stressful, and in my mind, I believed being a victim of police experiences was over. However, it appeared that the drama was just beginning.

On Friday, January 6, 1999, I was attending a Lakers basketball game party at Breakshot Sports Bar around 3:00 pm. Cars were parked everywhere, but I was able to find a legal parking space on the street, learning a lesson from the 1995 encounter with the overzealous officer that detained me. Prior to this day, my tags were stolen, and I had to go to court to fight the tickets received for not having the tags on my car. The judge gave me paperwork to place on my dashboard showing that my car was registered. I ensured the documents were visible to avoid any issues.

While inside watching the game for about an hour, the staff announced on the intercom that cars were being towed. For a moment, I hesitated because I knew I was legally parked and had paperwork validating my registration. However, just to be sure, I decided to check on my car as well.

As I exited the bar and looked on the street, I observed my vehicle being towed. Initially, I chased the tow truck down the street, but I could not catch it. Suddenly, a friend pulled up to attend the event, so I asked him to follow the tow truck. As it was being towed heading westbound on Washington Blvd from Inglewood Avenue, I noticed that my 1990 Infinity Q45 was being dragged with the tires at a forty-five-degree angle. At that point, I was concerned that my car was being damaged, so I asked my friend to speed and catch up with the truck. As soon as we were on the side of the driver, I waved to get his attention and asked him to roll down his window. I intended to let him know that he was damaging my car, but he never acknowledged my request…he just gestured for us to follow him. He made a left turn off Washington Blvd and moments later, we were at the gate of the tow yard, the official police tow yard for West Bureau.

I jumped out of my friend's ride, followed my car through the gate, and approached the driver. "Sir, you were towing my vehicle at a crooked angle!" He did not acknowledge my complaint, so I went on to say, "Can I get my paperwork out of the car?"

He said, "You need to go to the office."

"Did you see the paperwork on the dashboard?" I asked. "Yes," he replied.

"Let me get your business card," I interrupted while he was responding as I could see the paperwork in the dashboard. He handed me his card, and I proceeded to the office where I was met by an older Oriental lady.

"I need to get my paperwork out of the car, which verifies my car was towed by mistake." She gave me a permission removal slip, and I gave it to the driver and retrieved the documents. When I returned to the office, I presented the paperwork to the lady, letting her know that the documents were from a judge temporarily validating my registration. I went on to explain that my previous car tags were stolen.

She told me that there is nothing that she could do and I would need to speak to the owner, Joe. I asked her to call him right then, but she said that he would not be available until Monday. The tow yard was due to close in thirty- minutes, so I started making calls to the Department of Transportation but did not get through to anyone.

At that point, I decided to rush back to where my car was towed from because there was no way I wanted my car to be stuck in the tow yard the entire weekend. When I walked out of the office, I hitched a ride from a genuinely nice man who was just getting his car. I asked him to take me back to Breakshot, which was only about eight minutes away.

When I arrived at the sports bar, I asked the traffic officers, who were still towing cars and writing tickets, to contact a supervisor. Unfortunately, there wasn't one available, and the officers on site were not authorized to make a judgment call. Time had run out, and I had exhausted all means to get my car prior to Monday. So, I decided to enjoy the rest of my night and went back inside to join my friends, Marvin Brent and Steve Smith., who were also police officers.

Monday morning, I arrived at the Pacific Division Police Station and went to the front desk – I had the officer run my plates to see who had to release my car. I knew I would not be able to see the judge, and I wanted my car, so I did what I had to do. I was told that the Department of Transportation had a hold on my vehicle due to unpaid fees. I went to the DMV to pay all fees, and once I had all my receipts, I went back to the tow yard to obtain my vehicle.

When I arrived, I asked the cashier up front to speak to Joe, whose name I was given by the first lady I spoke to. The cashier, who identified herself as Shelley, said he was not there. I asked if the previous lady I spoke to was there as she was the one who told me that I need to ask for him.

Shelley, in an agitated tone, said, "No, neither of them are here. I'm the one who will help you. That's it!" Suddenly, the Oriental lady I talked to initially walked into the room from the back office. I asked Shelley, "I thought you said she wasn't here?"

Shelley really became agitated at that point because I had caught her in a bald-faced lie. I proceeded to show her the business card the other lady gave me, and for the first time, I mentioned to her that I am a former police officer while presenting my retired police identification, saying, "I understand the protocol, and I am not trying to be a problem. I just want to speak to the person who I was referred to."

She was really irritated again and stated, "If you are a police officer, I can get you in a lot of trouble!"

I responded, "I'm a retired officer, and you can't get me in nothing because I didn't do nothing."

She said a couple of more things related to getting me in trouble, and I responded back, "Look, you can't get me in shit! Just give me my car."

I paid for the tow, got my receipt, got in my car, and left the location.

Six months later, I was studying to take the final exam at West Coast Detectives to become a private detective. I had just left a study group, driving the same 1990 Infinity Q45 going southbound on La Cienega at the 405 freeway, when I was pulled over by LA County Sheriffs in a marked black and white. Upon approaching my vehicle, they asked for my driver's license, insurance, and registration.

As I was providing the information to the officer requested, I asked, "What am I being stopped for?"

The deputy replied, "You have a bad taillight."

I knew that he just got behind me from a side street, so I knew that was fabricated right off the bat, but I didn't say anything. I just let them do their jobs. After running my information through the computer, both deputies approached with an entirely different attitude. They had their guns out, pointing them at me and saying, "Get your hands up! Get your hands up!"

I put my hands up and asked, "For what? What did I do?" Answering my own question, I said, "I haven't done anything!" I was scared for my life!

They said, "Just shut up and keep your hands up and get out of the car."

I got out of the car and said, "Sir, I'm a retired police officer. I have not committed any crimes. Something has to be wrong!"

At this point, I was scared as hell because I had no idea why this was happening. I was handcuffed and put in the back of the police car. Ten minutes later, one of the sheriffs came and sat down in the front seat and said, "You have a warrant for your arrest."

"For what? I have never been arrested!"

He responded, "538PC, impersonating a police officer."

"Sir, I am a retired officer with a retired police identification." Desperate for them to realize this was a mistake, I said, "It's in my wallet in the front seat of my car."

He retrieved my ID, had a ten-minute conversation with his partner, and then he requested a supervisor. At that point, I had been handcuffed in the back of a police car for thirty minutes, and it took another twenty minutes for the sergeant to arrive.

At that point, I was irritated and confused, never once remembering the issue I had with Shelley at the tow yard who said, plain as day, she could get me in a lot of trouble.

The sergeant questioned me and concluded that it made no sense that a retired officer would ever need to impersonate a police officer, especially since I had a valid retired ID. After an hour, I was released. They gave me the information I needed to pursue the origin of the warrant, and then I was able to leave.

I moved on, passed my final exam that Friday, and immediately got in the mode to address the warrant that I did not know existed. That following Monday, I contacted my attorney, Winston McKesson, to find out how to address the issue. I was directed to turn myself into the LA Police Department on Sunday and serve time. I did as I was told, but the detectives said they would not book me for a misdemeanor and directed me to go to WLA Court at 9:00 am the next morning.

When I showed up to court, the judge was surprisingly upset with me. He said, "If you are late tomorrow or for any other court proceeding, you will be held in contempt of court and guilty of the crime charged."

I tried to explain and said, "This was the time I was told to arrive."

He said, "It doesn't matter, don't be late again!"

I went to court for several weeks straight when they finally dismissed my case, recognizing that it did not make sense that a retired officer would need to impersonate a police officer. So much time, pain, and stress because of a vindictive White lady who did not feel a Black man had any business questioning her. So, she did what she had probably gotten away with so many times…used her White privilege.

I filed a wrongful retaliatory complaint against the company that unjustifiably towed my car, and then to add insult to injury, an employee concocted a story…Jones vs. the tow yard. To this day, I have no idea as to the adjudication of the case. I believe that the attorney, which handled the lawsuit, took a deal to squash the case and left me hanging. I never got a resolution, but it was noted that the LA Police Department falsely gave the information for the warrant stating that I was fired, not retired.

A personal acquaintance that I inspired to join the police force and who I can no longer call a friend was working with the LA Police Department and knew about my case but never let me know. No one ever apologized or took the time to explain how this could happen. This was another majorly stressful situation that I experienced in my life, and I have no idea why. The woman, who falsely accused me of a crime, never paid for what she did.

CHAPTER 17

They Keep Messing with Me

"He stopped what he was doing and walked toward me while yelling, 'Shut the fuck up and mind your business!' When he got a few feet away, he pushed me."

On 25 January 1999, I threw a party for my son's eighth birthday. We had clowns, dancers, food, and music. At that time, we were probably the only African American family in the immediate neighborhood of predominately White affluent homeowners near Hancock Park in the Mid-Wilshire District. A little after 6:00 pm, a black and white police unit arrived and said they were called for a noise complaint. The music was too loud and needed to be turned down. Of course, we complied with the demand of the officers, making sure the noise level was acceptable.

The party continued for about another hour as the plan was to end at 8:00 pm. We kept the music at the same level that the officers requested, but around 7:45 pm, another unit pulled up with different officers and a female sergeant. I recognized her immediately as we were partners during my tenure at Wilshire two years prior.

I joyfully spoke to her, and she professionally spoke back, but then she went on to mention that there was a complaint earlier. I explained that the music was at the same level the initial officers requested and that the party was practically over. People were slowly leaving at that point, so we just turned the music off to avoid any problems. Based on her actions after that, I had to assume that she was privy to the false rumor spreading around the department a few years back about me taking a gang member's side over an officer. The reason I say that is to my surprise, the sergeant gave me a ticket for having a loud party. It was an extremely petty infraction with a hefty fine.

In my eight years of being an officer, I never cited or heard of anyone getting a fine for loud music unless it was completely out of hand, with a large crowd, traffic issues, fights, or problems of disturbance. I pondered for days how someone I knew and thought I got along with could come to my home and give me a ticket for something so minor. We used to ride in the same car…she was my partner. Where was the "Spirit of the Law?" Where was "We are all Blue?" No, I was not an active officer, but I was retired.

Later on, in the week, I received a phone call from a former friend at the division who stated she heard a female sergeant bragging about citing an Officer Jones for a noise violation, and she wanted to verify that it was me that the sergeant was talking about. Surprising to the officer, I confirmed that it was me. I must admit this situation hurt my feelings since harassing me was a joke to the sergeant. I could not wrap my mind around why she would do something like that, but I chose not to report it. I just sucked it up and said karma would come back on her. I think I heard later that she was fired.

I started to wonder if my name was floating around the police department like it did when I was still an active officer. It seemed that retaliation was underway, and the person who called for my head would not call off the force until I was dead or in prison.

I Promoted to Survive

My experiences as a police officer drove me to be one of the hottest promoters of social events in Los Angeles. My partners and I started with dances at hotels for the Los Angeles Police and Fire Departments, having a turnout of around a thousand working professionals. The money we made inspired me to host events once a month so that I could pay my bills and feed my family. Since so much was at stake, I had to promote efficiently and aggressively to guarantee success. I was so stressed out from all the encounters with the police force; I later realized that promoting kept me so busy providing an outlet of great vibes and that it kept me alive. It released my mind from the pain and disappointment that being a police officer gave me.

I always knew I would be involved in promotions or own a nightclub because my dad owned a banquet room called The Joneses Patio back in the early 70s. Music, fun, and good people…that's the way to make a living, although the road to promotions was a bumpy one as I was dealing with financial problems and litigation created by the LA Police Department.

If it were up to the Los Angeles Police Department, I would die a slow death through the torture of no work. Since leaving the police force, I have not been able to secure steady employment. I completed an application and got far in the process at multiple places, including USC Police, County Probation, Signal Hill Police Department, Cal State Police Department, and the list goes on. I applied, scored high on the testing, and ranked at the top of all applicants, and then later denied. Being blackballed impacts everything I try to do.

I was once a happy and successful person; however, after my experiences as a police officer, my life changed. Since retiring, things have become worse.

My former career, continuous harassment, and being blacklisted prohibited me from finding suitable employment, thus placing me in a financial bind. It is not like I do not want to work – I do.

There is no way for me to live on retirement alone. Out of the thirty percent of my previous income that I receive for retirement, I pay monthly for medical insurance, I have living expenses, and outstanding debt. On top of that, I have not received assistance for the injuries that occurred while on the job, even though I was told that I get medical coverage for life. Excruciating pain, my physical condition, and my increased weight all make it difficult for me to exercise. I realize that I need professional help with my situation.

Taco Tuesdays

After the multitude of negative things that I dealt with in the past, it seemed like the issues would never stop. Every Tuesday, I hosted Taco Tuesday at a Mexican Restaurant in South-Central Los Angeles. In September 2017, while hosting an event, I noticed that a police unit conducted a traffic stop on a car in the parking lot not far from the front door of the venue. I found out that the people they stopped were my business partner's niece and her husband.

After talking to the driver, the officer began searching the trunk of their car. I was around forty feet away, watching everything transpire, as I was standing with a group of people who were outside smoking cigarettes. So, I asked, "Did you give them permission to search your car?"

They both responded with, "No."

With around eight patrons witnessing the encounter, one of the officers who was searching the trunk, stopped what he was doing and walked aggressively toward me while yelling for me to "Shut the fuck up and mind your business!"

When he got a few inches away, he pushed me while I backed away at the same time.

I said to him, "What the fuck are you doing? Get your ass out of my face!" I continued to back away, and he kept coming for me.

He pushed me again and said, "Motherfucker, who do you think you are?"

"I was talking to my people! Get the fuck back! I know what your ass is trying to do."

At that point, his partner was making his way in our direction, yelling. I explained that I was the promoter of the event, and I was just making sure my customers were good. I said, "Bro, just leave me alone. I'm not stupid enough to fight you so you can shoot my ass!"

The officer, who appeared to be of a Spanish/Caucasian mix, said a few more words and then walked inside the restaurant, which was owned by Hispanics. He was inside for about five minutes, and I assumed he was talking to the owner's wife. When he came back outside, he approached me again, laughed as though it was funny, made a comment under his breath, went to his car, and left. I felt violated and was upset by his actions, so it was hard for me to get back into a good mood and enjoy the rest of the evening.

The next morning the owner of the restaurant called me and said, "Your event is canceled! We don't do business with people who don't respect the police."

In pure disbelief, I tried to plea my case and convince the owner that he was making a mistake. "Man, I'm a retired police officer, and I do respect the police. The guy was harassing our guests, and when I said something to the customers, the officer tried to bate me into a fight with him. He got frustrated when I did not fight him and told your wife I did something wrong." I continued to plead my case and went on to say, "We had multiple witnesses outside that saw him push me and bump up against me twice."

The owner unapologetically said, "The event is canceled."

Within a couple of days, I went to the 77th Division to report the incident. I felt it was my responsibility to report him as a regular citizen. If I was not trained and did not possess the self-discipline it takes to not respond to an aggressive officer, I would have fought him and ended up dead.

While there, I gave my initial statement to a sergeant, and it was later determined that the officer in question worked at the Metropolitan Division, a precinct where officers are supposed to be the best trained that the police force has to offer, and the same place where SWAT officers are trained. I was then told that they were requesting a Metropolitan Division Sergeant, and I would have to wait for his arrival.

After about an hour, the sergeant arrived, and I gave him a taped testimony of what occurred. Several months later, I received a letter in the mail stating there would be an investigation. About a year later, a lieutenant at Metro Division called and said that he was working on my case. It has been three years at this point, and I have not heard a word.

Being a Promoter for Versatile Prod kept me Sane

CHAPTER 18

My Quest to Stop a Killer

"I understood what he was going through and felt I could possibly reach him through the media in hopes to stop him from continuing the massive killing spree."

In early February 2013, about 3:00 am, I could not sleep as my heart was overwhelmed with grief and sympathy due to two of the supervisors' families were killed. The murders seemed to be targeted as police officers had been shot as well. The suspect was believed to be driving a "blue pickup truck" driven by a former police officer, Christopher Dorner. Numerous trucks that resembled Dorner's were mistakenly shot up by the police with occupants inside that looked nothing like their supposed suspect.

This situation had my PTSD kicking in on a high level, causing me to be extremely emotional. Yes, I was torn. I could empathize and understand what Officer Christopher Dorner may have been feeling after getting fired for doing the right thing. However, I felt far worse for the innocent lives he was taking. The added trauma occurred when I looked at his photo on the television screen as the news was consistently blasting his picture. I noticed that I had a common feature with Dorner…I am Black.

Prior to the unfortunate and sad situation, I had never spoken to, seen, or met the man and had been long retired when he started with the force. Outside of being concerned for innocent bystanders, I didn't want to be mistakenly shot by officers in fear for their life – Christopher and I resembled each other at a glance.

I understood what he was going through and felt that I could possibly reach him through the media in the hopes of stopping him from continuing the massive killing spree. What I was heartbroken and surprised about was how the media pushed their own agenda, saying that I somehow sided with Dorner. That pissed me off and caused me to shut down. The way things were being reported put me in danger; in fear for my life, I stopped talking to reporters.

Subsequently, I received death threats and hate messages due to the media's false assessment of my manifesto's true intent. All I wanted was for Dorner to stop killing and for the police force to look at how they treated their officers. I wanted to be part of the reform; instead, the same issues I wrote about are still present today.

To give you an idea of the atrocities imposed on Black officers in the police department, I remind you of Christopher

Dorner, a former police officer, who in 2013, murdered others in an effort to clear his name. You can find his entire manifesto online and witness how he could no longer handle the treatment and humiliation he felt was unjustly inflicted on him. This was a man who, prior to being an officer, served in the United States Navy and carried his name with honor. In his detailed proclamation, Dorner addressed America, named the offenders, and offered an explanation as to why he was acting what many said was out of his character. He even said that his actions were his "Last Resort," as indicated in the subject line of his address.

After acting on what he said he would do, Dorner wrote:

"I know most of you who personally know me are in disbelief to hear from media reports that I am suspected of committing such horrendous murders and have taken drastic and shocking actions in the last couple of days. You are saying to yourself that this is completely out of character of the man you knew who always wore a smile wherever he was seen. I know I will be vilified by the LA Police Department and the media. Unfortunately, this is a necessary evil that I do not enjoy but must partake and complete for substantial change to occur within the police department and reclaim my name. The department has not changed since the Rampart and Rodney King days. It has gotten worse. The consent decree should never have been lifted. The only thing that has evolved from the consent decree is those officers involved in the Rampart scandal and Rodney King incidents that have since been promoted to supervisor, commanders, and command staff, and executive positions. The question is, what would you do to clear your name?"

After reading this, I realized that he and I had the same experiences. The fact that I left the force in 1997 and lived over a decade without considering retaliation against those that did me wrong made me fall to my knees, thanking God for keeping me in my right mind. The officers who once called me friend and brother smeared my name too. To experience bullying and harassment as an officer is something that most cannot fathom. However, I am sure many others have had to take total abuse and dare not say a word about it. Only this time, Chris refused to be quiet. He wanted the world to feel his pain. He went on to share the importance of your name and how it is a reflection of your life and your legacy.

"My name is Christopher Dorner and I am very well known in my community. Evidently, it was also known around the police department, even outside of the precinct I was assigned to. If I wanted a negative connotation associated with my name, I could have very well chosen to be in the streets, like some of the people I grew up with. However, it was important to me to be an upstanding citizen with a positive contribution to society. Being an officer was supposed to be a badge of honor, but instead it was a constant reminder of the significant pain that I experienced in life, and I am not sure why."

Reading Officer Dorner's story was almost like experiencing Deja vu, only I never considered responding as he did. I wasn't killing myself, nor was I killing anybody else. I just kept my composure when approached, and continuously figured out a way to survive…even when it was extremely difficult. My experiences seemed to mirror his. Dorner reported an officer for excessive force, Dorner was retaliated against, and I too experienced retaliation.

He mentioned that he broke the department's "Blue Line." He was fired. I retired due to the treatment I was receiving before they could fire me. He was accused of lying to an officer, and I was accused of taking a gang member's side, which was completely untrue. Sadly, the similarities let me know that this is repeated behavior, and I am almost certain it continues to occur in the Los Angeles Police Department today. And the question that is always asked is: "Why don't officers say something when they see something?"

You may believe that race has nothing to do with the mistreatment we experienced during our stint in what used to be a respected occupation, but I would argue that I never witnessed one White officer ending up in a similar situation. With the sweeping under the rug, turning a blind eye, and denying actual events that occurred, I would say to every officer that participates exactly what Christopher Dorner wrote when the detectives from Internal Affairs investigated a situation he was involved in. He wrote, "only (1) officer (unknown) in the van other than myself had statements consistent with what actually happened. The other six officers all stated they heard nothing and saw nothing. Shame on every one of you."

A lot of thought and manipulation goes into making sure that the life of an ostracized officer is ruined. To get numerous fellow officers to lie in court after swearing to tell the truth must be a result of threats and fear. The shock, disbelief, and heart-wrenching pain associated with methodically discrediting you as a person and as an officer of the law is mind-blowing. I am not sure that I will ever overcome the mental anguish associated with the strategic planning of my demise.

As I mentioned when I started to tell my story, my life, my health, and my relationships, they were never the same after I joined the Los Angeles Police Department. When you lie, bully, harass, verbally assault, and intentionally ruin a person for the sake of brotherhood, you are no better than the gang members who you approach in the streets. You are no better than an abuser in a domestic violence situation. You are no better than a murderer, and you are no better than a serial rapist, continuing to fuck those that are upstanding and moral. You have ruined entire families for generations to come, and I do not understand how you can sleep at night.

Driven over the edge, Christopher continued to explain his choices: "I have exhausted all available means at obtaining my name back. I have attempted all legal court efforts within appeals at the Superior Courts and California Appellate courts. This is my last resort. The LA Police Department has suppressed the truth, and it has now led to deadly consequences. Their actions have cost me my law enforcement career that began on 2/7/05 and ended on 1/2/09. They cost me my Naval career, which started on 4/02 and ends on 2/13. I had a TS/SCI clearance (Top Secret Sensitive Compartmentalized Information clearance) up until shortly after my termination with the police force. This is the highest clearance a service member can attain other than a Yankee White TS/SCI, which is only granted for those working with and around the President/Vice President of the United States. I lost my position as a Commanding Officer of a Naval Security Forces reserve unit at NAS Fallon because of the LA Police Department. I've lost a relationship with my mother and sister because of the police force. I've lost a relationship with close friends because of the police force. In essence, I've lost everything because the LA Police Department took my name and knew I was INNOCENT!!!"

If Christopher Dorner was crazy as the media and police department led you to believe, he would not have been so detailed about every deplorable encounter he experienced from the LA Police Department, along with every honorable position he held and badge he proudly wore. Today, we continue to fight for the same thing...honor, respect, and the truth. As Americans, we are supposed to be equal, but for some reason, Black men in America have to fight for equality and respect. Chris reminded us:

"I am an American by choice. I am a son. I am a brother. I am a military service member. I am a man who has lost complete faith in the system since the system betrayed, slandered, and libeled me. I lived a good life, and though not a religious man, I always stuck to my own personal code of ethics, ethos and always stuck to my shoreline and true North."

I could go on and on, pulling exact quotes from Christopher Dorner's manifesto, but I don't want to be misunderstood as being supportive of his actions. My intent is to point out the facts to those who will listen and hopefully to those who have the power to make a change. The most recent deaths of George Floyd and Breonna Taylor, and the outrage that their murders caused, are additional evidence that the way the departments operate plays a major role in all the unnecessary fatalities. They are not former officers, but they were citizens that deserved to live.

The Intent of My Manifesto

When I wrote my manifesto, I had no idea that it would be perceived in a negative way – I sincerely wanted to help. Thinking, like a negotiator, that the former officer, now deceased suspect, would realize that his way of dealing with injustice was not the right way. I wanted him to value life like I value life, and I wanted him to realize that the death of the innocent was not going to create the change he was looking for.

Seven years have passed, and the badge still seems to be a license to harass, antagonize, provoke, beat, and worst of all, kill with no consequences. When reading my words, I implore readers to take a step back and understand that I want everyone to be happy and healthy and be treated with respect and dignity.

As you read my manifesto that was written in 2013, I implore you to engage and feel the conviction behind each word I wrote back then. I would never agree or side with anyone that seeks revenge by murdering innocent people – I wanted to be a part of the change, and I thought telling the truth would be a great start.

By Former Police Officer Joe Jones MANIFESTO… Written and published February 2013

I know most of you who know me personally are in disbelief of the partial story I will tell today—a story that has been suppressed for about eighteen years but lives strong every day of my life.

I, without hesitation, would like to send my condolences to the victims who were lost and their families during this tragic situation. I would also like to send my condolences and well wishes to the many former and current officers, as well as citizens and their families who lost the lives and souls of loved ones to the injustices of police corruption, scandal, lies, deception, and brutality.

Unlike Former Officer Dorner, I fear dying, but I also fear living in a society where innocent people are dying for no reason. A society where pain so great can be afflicted on people who have a desire to live right, treat people right, and then be punished for doing right.

They say we all look alike – in very few cases, this, of course, is true – but in most cases, it is not. I feel a resemblance to Dorner (See Photos). However, several people who have no resemblance to Dorner have been shot due to the fear of what is taking place. I DO NOT WANT TO BE SHOT FOR CRIMES. I DID NOT COMMIT!

Neither does anyone else.

To preface my story, I will say this: Just like former Officer Christopher Dorner, I used to smile a lot. I loved everyone. I was voted friendliest senior of my Sr. Class in high school. I always believed in the system and never got into any trouble. I loved hard and gave all I could. After joining the police force in 1989, I quickly found out that the world and society had major flaws. I had flaws as well, forever believing that our system of government was obligated to do the right thing. This is what I believed as a young officer. Without going into major detail, I need you to first assume that I would not surface sixteen years later with lies about a situation that has me with PTSD to this very day. The pain forces me to speak as I have yet to shake the ills of my experience as a police officer. Of course, I have moved on physically, but mentally and emotionally, I still live with flaws.

I cannot go into re-living the emotions of what I went through, so I will say this. I had my home viciously attacked by a gunman with my family and myself inside the house. No arrests were made, and my family and I received little support. I had my Civil Rights violated on several occasions. I was falsely arrested at gunpoint by the sheriffs as an officer who identified himself and was conspired against by both the LA Police Department and the sheriffs when my civil case went to trial. I was falsely accused on more than one occasion and simply placed in a position that the trust was so compromised that I could no longer wear the uniform. Also, know there were many more episodes.

All of these issues are well documented, and I present them not to be a whistleblower but hoping that one would not assume that all of what is being said are lies, as presented by Dorner. I don't know him, but I know me.

I will say, from my experience, if a person knows they were wrong, it is easier to move on without anger. It seems that Dorner obviously could not move on…Could I just be content and move on with my life and not say anything? Yes… then I would feel that I, for once, had my chance to speak on something that hurts me to this day, and I did nothing to arouse thought or provoke reform.

This is what I hope comes from this whole situation:

1. Families who lost someone to this tragedy find the peace that only God can give at this terrible time.

2. Citizens of Los Angeles be mindful of this fearful time to be an officer and comply vigorously so that you are not the victim of an officer on high alert.

3. Government and politicians please be diligent in the responsibility of creating laws that protect those that could be the victim of a conspiracy. Never allow the door to be shut on the truth.

4. Honest and Fair LA Police Officers & All Agencies: Keep doing what you are doing to protect citizens and be safe while you are doing so. We need you, and I would hope that you do not allow the bureaucratic drama and stress to kill your morale as I know it can.

5. Unethical LA Police & All Agencies: Whatever it was that leads you down this path, pray to somebody's God to forgive you and begin to remove unethical methods to your policing style. Always think, what if it were you, how would you feel? How would you like if you were falsely accused and your life, livelihood, and career were taken from you? How would you like it if someone were beating on you just because they felt they could get away with it? You are no better than the criminals you took an oath to arrest when you do what you do!

6. Christopher Dorner. The first thing I would say to him is, I feel your pain! But you are going about this the wrong way. To take innocent lives could never be the answer to anything. I say this as a man who experienced the same pain, betrayal, anger, suffering, litigation, and agony that you did in many ways, only I did not get fired. I just chose to go a different route. My heart still suffered that same shock. I was still left to try and put the pieces back together. The disbelief that people could conspire and cause you to lose something you loved so dearly was still there. I lost my career, I lost my family, I lost my dignity, I lost my trust...but I am here now to hopefully one day see change... Bro, don't kill any more innocent people. Your point has been made. Clearly, they know you mean business. The whole world knows. Refrain

from any further wrongdoing and do what you must in order to salvage your soul. Whatever that means to you. Just remember that God is a forgiving God.

In conclusion, I say to people who knew none of this about me that one day I would have to reflect on when was the time to speak. When I see the potential for innocent lives to be lost…the time is now!

Joe Jones

Although the thought of wearing a police uniform affected me, I had to repair my life and live for my children. Unlike Christopher Dorner, I did not believe life could no longer go on. I was angry as hell but would have never thought to kill anyone due to my experience as an officer. I wanted so bad to be a good officer with a respected career, but somehow, they kept coming for me.

Article in US News written by Seth Cline, Senior Producer, News. Feb 13, 2013, https://www.usnews.com/news/articles/2013/02/13/christopher-dorners-criticisms-were-valid-ex-cops-say

THE MANHUNT FOR Christopher Dorner caught the attention of the nation, but for some, the contents of Dorner's manifesto may be what people remember about the tragedy for years to come.

Several supporters, many of them former minority law enforcement themselves, have backed the claims Dorner made in his lengthy screed. In the manifesto, Dorner focused on the racism and corruption he witnessed in the Los Angeles Police Department he would go on to terrorize.

Then there was the article from BET News written by Natelege Whaley, February 14, 2013, https://www.bet.com/news/national/2013/02/14/two-black-cops-write-statements-about-racism-in-lapd.html#!

Two Black Cops Write Statements About Racism in LAPD

Sgt. Wayne K. Guillary and former officer Joe Jones are speaking up about their own experiences with racism in the LAPD, in light of Dorner's killings.

Sgt. Wayne K. Guillary and former officer Joes Jones are speaking up about racism in the LAPD. (Photos from left: twitter/4topcat, Facebook/JoeJones)

Christopher Dorner is believed to have died in a burning cabin Tuesday, according to The Los Angeles Times. The ex-LAPD cop was wanted for killing three people, including a police officer.

Before Dorner's shooting spree, he wrote a manifesto explaining that his rage was motivated by racism he faced from childhood until being fired from the LAPD. Sgt. Wayne K. Guillary, a Black LAPD officer, and Joe Jones, a former one, are opening up about their own experiences with racism in the police department.

They support Dorner's belief that the LAPD needs reform, but had also asked Dorner to stop the killings.

CHAPTER 19

Now This

"I plead Not Guilty. In my heart, I feared allowing my fate to be determined by a Public Defender."

On December 15, 2019, I was due to support my son at his performance in a concert called Rolling Loud, which was being held at Banc of California Stadium next to the Coliseum. I was supposed to be picked up from my house in a sprinter van by my son and his manager. At around 12:15 pm, they called and told me they were running late and that I should meet them at the gate, and they would wait for me by the artist's entrance. I had a choice of two cars but realized one of my cars did not have gas in it, so I took my other one. It was a last-minute, spontaneous decision.

Upon arrival, my son's manager was at the blocked entrance and gave me a parking pass to park in the lot while their party started exiting the sprinter van in front of the entrance gate. I proceeded to park in the lot, but as I approached the garage, I was suddenly directed to pull to the right by a security officer, a hundred feet from the entrance. Suddenly, I was told to turn off my vehicle and get out of my car.

Of course, I asked why? Suddenly, and without my permission, another female security guard with a dog rapidly approached my vehicle, then started circling my car with no explanation. They opened my back doors and let the dog in my backseat. The dog sniffed around while the female guard put her hand under my passenger side seat and removed my handgun, which was loaded and in a holster. It was at that point I realized that the day before I had family members with kids coming to visit, I always put the gun in the car for safekeeping. I totally forgot it was there.

The female officer then called for the Sergeant and then asked for my ID and retired police ID. I immediately told them I did not realize the gun was there. "I got in this car last minute to see my son's performance." They began to talk among each other and called for an additional unit of two officers to transport me to the Southwest Station.

While in route, the officers were saying this should not have happened, and they would probably release me. Once at Southwest station, the officer placed me on the bench in handcuffs, where I sat for an hour. Then a sergeant came out and started asking me questions. Subsequently, he let me know that I was not being booked, but my gun would be kept until I saw the detectives within a few days.

After another thirty minutes, they gave me a receipt for my gun and a business card. The officers returned me to the stadium, but by then, my son's performance was over. The entire process took about two and a half hours. I was baffled as it all happened so quickly.

The following week I went to the Southwest Station in hopes of retrieving my gun but was told by the detective on duty that I had to talk to the detective in charge of gun detail. I attempted to reach him by phone and was unable to. No one seemed to know who exactly was handling my issue. However, about two months later, the gun detective called me. He asked me questions about my ID and other guns registered to me. I then asked him questions as I was worried at that point after being told that I would likely be able to pick up my gun.

After we talked for a few minutes, he said he was submitting a report to the city attorney, and they would be the ones who would decide what action would be taken. I was really confused then as this unforeseen incident appeared to not be going away.

One month after that call, I received a letter dated March 25, 2020, stating I was being charged for carrying a loaded firearm PC25850a. At that point, I was really beginning to feel like I was dealing with a serious issue, contrary to the fact every police officer, detective, and attorney I spoke to said it would be nothing. But somehow, here I am, facing an arraignment.

In the Criminal Courts Building on July 14, 2020, at 8:30 am, I learned from a public defender that I was offered a plea deal. They offered sixty days in jail, forty-five days of Cal Trans detail, or three years of probation. I plead not guilty. In my heart, I feared allowing my fate to be determined by a public defender offering me a plea. I just simply feel they work in concert with the courts and make deals instead of vigorously fighting for their client's freedom.

To this day, I am still dealing with this case after hiring a very well- respected trial lawyer. Here I am, fifty-five years old, never been arrested, with no criminal record. I was a police officer for eight years, and I have a security guard card. The only reason I don't have a renewed gun permit is because of the slow-down in background checks due to COVID. The whole thing was foul and uncalled for, being that I did not give anyone permission, nor did they have a valid reason to search my car in the first place. Where I do take responsibility is for the fact that I forgot to take a loaded gun that is registered to me out of the car. Lord knows I don't want to go to jail for something like this. I would rather have knowingly committed a crime than gone through something like this simply for forgetting. It is now December of 2020, and I am still fighting for my freedom as it pertains to this case.

CHAPTER 20

Color Blind

"I have been a victim of police misconduct as a teen, an educated black man, a black LA police officer, and a retired LA police officer."

My life and career were ruined by the police force, and I am speaking my peace because I continue to live the nightmares. However, I would never want to live in this world without the police. I do not hate the police, but I despise the mentalities of those who abuse their power. It is time for a change. Let go of the hate, ego, and ungodly principles that make you believe you are better than someone simply because you are a different color and because you simply do not understand them. Everybody is tired. Your own children are tired.

There was no greater joy than to see the BLM movement during the recent George Floyd riots and see that the protesters were of all colors and nationalities. They get it!

It's time for the Brass of the various police departments and political leaders to get it! Reform and change must happen now. I am not a spokesman for all people. However, being on both sides gives me a vantage point that forces me to speak to you with love in my heart for the many victims of police brutality and racial injustice. Then I must speak to the officers who are in command and as well as officers who have arrived at a place of a lack of care, understanding, and respect for victims and officers with darker skin than you.

For change to occur, firstly, revert to a standard principle that all humans were created equal. Now treat all encounters as such. Create laws and procedures that eliminate ways for the poor or minorities to be preyed against. Force officers to tape-record all encounters with citizens and eliminate any excuses or options to forgo this process. Enforce automatic termination if the video is not utilized. Renew civilian review boards with a special section of Black supervising officers, citizens, and politicians that review the tactics of any officer involved in a racial incident.

Reward officers for treating people with dignity when force could have been an option. Force officers to have personal intervention and counsel sessions with Black families, gang members, students, and professionals for eighty hours before they can patrol the streets of the city they work. All officers must work foot-beats in Black areas for four weeks per year, and this includes supervisors and detectives. All officers must have four hours of sensitivity training of Black officers and Black citizens per month.

They need to know more about the people they police and work with. Monitor the racial make-up of the traffic stops and citations written by all officers to detect if they have a pattern of injustice. Any claimed accidental shootings racial in nature, where no weapon is found, or no immediate threat to life is detected, is an automatic termination and prosecution of said officer. Three strikes on all racial incidents with no injuries. Document all racial encounters. If more than two are unjustified, the officer is automatically suspended for two months without pay. On the third, the officer is terminated. As it pertains to the Board of Rights for Black Officers, they are entitled to have an equal number of Black supervisors as other supervisors.

As things currently exist, all officers who have displayed a pattern of questionable shootings or beyond five racially charged incidents be terminated immediately. All officers must change divisions every three years. Specialized units must transfer every five years. All officers and supervisors must see a psyche every three years and be evaluated for stress, anger, and PTSD. Being a Los Angeles police officer should involve the entire city. It gives no officer an opportunity to develop consistent patterns or opportunities of oppressing people of a particular walk of life.

Lastly, reinstate the consent decree. As a former officer, I say, once again, I am not against the police. The police are tactical geniuses at dealing with crime and life or death situations when dealing with hardcore criminals. Our conversation is not about the real work police do. I'm against the police and courts who have used their authority to oppress, illegally incarcerate, brutalize or kill millions of Blacks. I don't wish to defund the police. I wish for enhanced training as it pertains to dealing with the stress of the job and a better understanding of dealing with Blacks.

As I've said before, I do not wish for the Department to be defunded. We have to keep in mind that the greater portion of officers have the right mentality, and the few bad apples spoil it for the bunch. I think other measures can be taken to change the overall philosophy of police departments nationwide. Police enlists to be officers, risking their lives and focus on serving the communities, then they are quickly encouraged and brainwashed into promoting for higher salaries and working in specialized units, as well as manning jobs civilians can do and frown on those who simply execute the most dangerous and important part of the job: Fighting crime on patrol.

Until the luster and financial reward for being a street cop are restored, officers nationwide will continue to do police work with hatred in their hearts, causing more lapses in judgment when dealing with citizens. This approach will continue to kill the moral of doing police work, and the streets will be filled with officers who simply do not cherish their jobs. If officers were paid appropriately for fighting crime as opposed to being promoted to jobs behind a desk and being rewarded, the overall mystique of an officer's mentality would change. Paying officers better hold them accountable. Don't defund them. Don't let the criminals get the upper hand. That will equal chaos.

I also implore Blacks to always do what is right. Good, fair police officers simply want to go home to their families safe every night. Always make their job easy whenever possible. The problem is that so many have done right, but due to fear, false arrest, death, or simply not knowing their rights, they don't speak on crimes by the police against them or that they never had a chance.

I hope my objective is clear. At the very least, I'm participating in the conversation for reform that will help police and Black citizen relations. No more pain, crying, and nightmares for me. No more silence. I am now sharing my TRUTH FOR CHANGE!

LAST THOUGHTS

Being forthcoming and basically spilling my guts to the world makes me realize that I must dedicate this book to everyone who has an interest in equality and due process for all people. The burdens I carried for over twenty years are finally being released. Although it took a lot of prayers, along with self-evaluation, to ensure that this book reflects my true intent of justice instead of revenge, I continue to ask God for guidance. The weight lifted off my shoulders from sharing sensitive information may bring different emotions depending on who you are. You may feel compassion, love, hate, resentment, or even be stunned depending on your background or level of awareness.

To Family & Friends

During my transgressions and dealings with the LAPD, I know that I was a pain in the ass to deal with. Hopefully, this book will provide you with a complete understanding as to why the person you knew before is no longer in your life. I am confident that you believe my heart is and will be the same.

However, it was encased in the hell that I went through with my employer and the circumstances that emerged with being a police officer. Your support, even when it was hard, does not go without true appreciation. I know that I have people in my life who genuinely love me, and that is why I live today!

To the Chief & Staff of LA Police

Power is a beautiful thing when it is not used for personal gain or self- gratification. In order to support those who trust and believe in you, it would be beneficial for all involved to leave your egos at home since it pertains to life- altering decisions you make that seriously impact human beings.

Replace nonsense with common sense, negligence and chaos with discipline and structure, and unfair discriminatory actions with ethics, integrity, and morals. Learn more about the officers you lead and the citizens you protect. More importantly, make all disciplinary actions even across the board. How can you guide me if you don't know me? How can you be trusted if you have no compassion for those you swore to lead and protect?

I ask that you seek and continue to elevate officers with integrity who properly protect, serve, and do not condone excessive force, mistreatment, assault, and murder. Because of the actions of fellow officers, all in blue are too hated and ridiculed as if they are the offenders themselves. Like me, you have encountered the victims and their families of all races, who have been subjected to the excruciating pain resulting from the actions of hateful officers and a corrupt system they believed was designed to protect them.

To Everyone Else

God has elevated me as a person while dealing with trials and tribulations that taught me valuable lessons...Some say I should not speak so candidly due to my status in the public eye. To those people, I say I have greater responsibility, and that is to tell the truth. GOD has a greater purpose for me, and because of that, I will speak.

I, like every other good-hearted American, have so much pain in my heart from the recent major incidents involving the police. Michael Brown, Eric Garner, Travon Martin, Oscar Grant, Sandra Bland, Breonna Taylor, and George Floyd are just some of the tragic situations that require me to use my voice in the hopes of bringing about change.

I can still see the beating of Rodney King that happened many years ago. It feels like it will never stop. Therefore, the victims of brutality and mistreatment can never stop shedding light as we cannot stand by and allow immoral and unethical behavior to continue. When I was an officer, I saw things that I thought were mishandled and still believe were wrong.

It must be known that we will not stand by and overlook misconduct. Fair punishment must be rendered to those who abuse their power. Officers, prosecutors, city attorneys, and judges must be accountable for the verdicts rendered from the courtrooms. Maybe then, officers of the law will not be so quick to beat innocent people and pull the trigger as part of the hunt of the Black man. A badge or a gavel does not make you God.

SPECIAL THANKS

There are numerous special people that played an integral part in who I am today. Without the family, relationships, battles, trials, tribulations, laughs, and tears, I would not have anything to share. My story is intended and will hopefully serve as an agent of change and as a therapy that will help me overcome the mental anguish associated with my career as a police officer. Some of the significant people include but are not limited to:

Joe E Jones Sr. – My father who taught me how to be a man and worked me extremely hard so that I would never want to work in construction like him. The support he gave me at a critical time in my life saved me from the gangs and drugs that were becoming an increasingly rapid issue in Los Angeles. He helped pave my way through school in San Diego, made sure I was away from our terrible neighborhood, and he would drive to San Diego to see my baseball games every weekend from Los Angeles.

Minnie B. Jones – My mother who, recently passed, was a kind, loving, and spiritual woman and worked extremely hard and allowed me to be a man in my early teens. Like most mothers, she was influential in building my character. Having responsibility gave me tons of confidence in life.

My Big Sisters – Sharon, Rose & Andrica – If it were not for you, I would probably have been afraid to stand up for myself. You gave me Heart! Love you all!

My Cousins – The Joneses on 93rd St. – All of you gave me confidence in everything I accomplished, from Baseball to being an officer. I love these cousins and all of my family!

Michele Roberson – My person who has given me unconditional love and stability over the past eighteen years. She dealt with the emotions of my PTSD and anger. I value and love you dearly for being the special person that you are.

Cynthia Jones – My ex-wife and mother of my children, who was more than likely the person I hurt most with the stress from the job and the many life experiences we endured together. She was loyal to me and did a fine job being a mother to our kids and a wife to such a troubled person.

Ms. Leona Smith – (Ex-Wife's Mother RIP) During the period I was in the Academy and in subsequent years, she took care of me like I was her own son. I will never forget her.

Michael Strawberry – Michael served as the driver for Chief of Police and was the first and only police officer that I knew personally at the time I was interested. He made me believe I could be a police officer.

Ralph Durham – He was a security officer at my high school that I grew close to. Ralph became a big brother to me and showed me what it looked like to be a family man. He gave me plenty of advice to help me keep my head on straight. From the age of thirteen years old up until today, we are still close.

Dennis Watsabaugh – My boss at HCB Contractors (Project Manager) who supported my every move in becoming an officer. He is a long-time family friend with a heart of gold.

Jonae Jones – My daughter, who was my inspiration to get my life on track as a young man, who was not sure what he wanted to do.

Corey and Casey Jones – My sons who make me extremely proud, kept me sane, and made life worth living. Sometimes, when I was not sure about myself, they forced me to man up.

Sgt. Doug Miller – Was the first Black sergeant that I worked for on probation in the West Valley Division. He looked out for me in a division that was not used to having Blacks.

Sgt. Daniel Mulrinen – You treated me as fair as any sergeant I ever worked for. Police work was the job I signed up for, and it was apparent when I was working for you.

The Three Amigos – Officer Marvin Brent (Class Leader in Academy), and Officer Eric "Tree" Moore, and I were The Three Amigos. They helped me through the academy. The fun and the competition made it a good experience. I love these guys!

Sgt. Jerry Stokes – My class drill instructor in the academy, who instilled the discipline I needed to get through tough times. I still admire and respect him as he never let me pass one inspection, which caused me razor bump agony. However, because of him, I passed my final inspection. What a man!

Hank Gathers and John "Chris" Brown – Both friends, deceased now, encouraged me through the process of the academy and gave me extreme joy during my times as a young officer. I still live with the pain of their passing. RIP!

CPSIA information can be obtained
at www.ICGtesting.com
Printed in the USA
FSHW012116020921

9 781736 328804